SOLICITOR
from HOME

Memories of a country lawyer in 1970's England

MELANIE RUSSELL

Copyright © 2014 Melanie Russell

The right of Melanie Russell to be identified as the author of this work has been asserted by her in accordance with the Copyright, Designs and Patents Act 1988. May all who read this book be richly blessed.

Published by Touchworks Ltd.
a company registered in England, no. 03668464.
Registered Office: 67 London Road, St. Leonards-on-Sea,
East Sussex TN37 6AR.

All rights reserved.

No part of this publication may be reproduced, stored in a retrieval system, or transmitted, in any form or by any means, electronic, mechanical, photocopying, recording or otherwise, without the prior permission of the copyright owner.

All the characters in this book are fictitious. Any resemblance to actual persons, living or dead, is purely coincidental.

A catalogue record for this title is available from The British Library.

Melanie Russell is a pseudonym

To Romney Marsh

A place whose wide flat lands and endless skies provide an inviting canvas for those who paint with the written word

And to

Those members of the Legal Profession across the world who take action, in small ways and large, so that evil does not prosper.

LUX GENTIUM LEX

'Law is the Light of the People'

Preface

This book is written as a fictionalised memoir.

I have recorded events that are as green in my memory as the first growth of last year's Spring. But, of course, no memoir can be truly accurate. I cannot truly remember the day that I noticed the first of last year's daffodils. I remember their beauty, the differing shapes of their trumpets and their colours, from deepest gold to palest cream, and I remember their fluid motion as the breeze set them dancing. But of the exact date, or whether it was sunshine, rain, wind or snow and what I was doing when I first noticed those daffodils, I have no idea.

All that remains in my memory is the composite feeling the sight of their beauty engendered in me through my senses: the memory is as much a spiritual connection with the beauty of Nature as it is of time and place, light and dark, smell, taste, touch, sight and hearing.

No memoir can be accurate, as it must be coloured by the writer's emotional links to her subject matter and the one-sided view of all situations which must perforce be the case in any such endeavour. Because of the lapse of time — and in this case nearly forty years have passed since the events I have recalled — I have taken the liberty of embroidering my story.

The silken fabric of a small country town set in green fields beneath wide skies has been embellished with the lazy-daisy stitch of a long hot summer, the smooth satin stitch of reminiscence, the herring-bone stitch that blends two stories into one, and the French knots of dialogue.

The whole becomes a patchwork quilt of sun and shade, joy and laughter, pain and sadness, hemmed with the broad blanket stitch of remembrance. The quilt is padded with times-and-customs-gone-by and it is kept in place by the buttons of nostalgia that secure the holes in my memory: holes that are well edged with button-hole stitch so that they do not fray.

I offer them as a gift from the country town where I first learned how the law impacts on everyday life and from the beautiful, atmospheric, wide open space that is Romney Marsh — above which my heart forever soars.

- 1 -

Well! You could have knocked me down with a feather.

My head felt as light and insubstantial as thistledown as I stumbled down the two steps from the Bank. I was only saved from an undignified trip by the collision of my extended stomach with the old black Ford motorcar parked outside.

The baby lurched and kicked hard against my diaphragm, depriving me of my remaining breath. Gasping for air, I hunched protectively forward over my pregnant belly while I concentrated on my breathing. A strong hand grasped my elbow and another patted my back reassuringly.

"Are you okay, Melanie?" asked the warm voice of Myles, the local doctor, whose particular interest was obstetrics and who had been in charge of my ante-natal care for the past eight months.

"I'm fine!" I said, feeling a chuckle start deep within as I looked up into his concerned eyes. I struggled to contain it, the effort sucking my breath away again, but to no avail. Soon I was laughing and Myles' mouth stretched into a mystified smile. "Mr Standish has ... has ..." It was no use, the whole situation was so ridiculous that I was lost for words.

"Yes? Mr Standish has ... what?" prompted Myles, his eyes now shining with amusement.

I did my best to explain. "I came to ask for an overdraft while I took maternity leave and Mr... Mr St... Mr Standish ..." Laughter threatened to overwhelm me again. I closed my eyes, and tried to pull myself together.

"Just breathe slowly and deeply," Myles advised, patting me on the back. "What's causing all this hilarity? I can't believe Mr Standish is the only cause."

I blinked hard and took a deep breath, but I had no hope of stifling my grin. "Mr Standish agreed," I said.

Myles looked puzzled. "I can understand that you're relieved about that! But surely there must be something else?"

"Oh yes, there is! " I schooled my features into a frown but it didn't stay long. The grin was back in an instant. "Mr Standish says that a solicitor is needed here in Oldchurch."

"Yes, that's true," Myles agreed. "In fact, I have something legal I'd like to run past you."

"No, no, no! I'm giving up work to have the baby. It's something I've always wanted."

"So why all the laughter?"

"Mr Standish said he'd find a baby-minder for the baby! It hasn't even been born yet! Not only that, he said he knew someone who would like to be my secretary."

"So he's organising you? I'm not surprised. It's his forté."

"I know, he's always very helpful. But finding me an office, a secretary, and a baby-minder — all in less than five minutes — is more than enough."

"*Has* he done more, then?" Myles chuckled, appreciating Mr Standish's skill in manipulating people.

"That's just it! Somehow I've agreed to make Wills for some of the bank's customers."

"That's tremendous!"

"Well, it would be helpful *eventually*, I agree. But Mr

SOLICITING FROM HOME

Standish has managed to fill my diary with clients for *tomorrow*!" Laughter — a rather desperate laughter — bubbled up again. "And the house is upside-down! It's always a mess by Friday. I'll have to be up very early tomorrow."

"I know you'll manage," Myles assured me.

Another thought occurred to me — and I struck the roof of the Ford with my fist in frustration: "Oh dear! I haven't asked the firm if I can do work from home. I hadn't even considered it."

Myles opened the car door which, as usual, I'd left unlocked. "It's a good thing this is your car," he commented drily. "Or you lawyers would say that was criminal damage! I suggest you drive back to Rye and clear the situation with your employers before you do yourself some damage, too."

- 2 -

Before I leap forward into the future let me take this opportunity to tell you a little of my past.

In 1976, when I received this amazing offer from my bank manager in response to a simple request for an overdraft, I was twenty seven years of age and expecting my first baby in a matter of weeks.

As one of the baby boomers born a couple of years after the end of the Second World War, I had benefitted from a very good and free secondary education at a girls' grammar school. When it came to choosing a subject to study at university, I was keen to find something other than the usual arts degree that traditionally led to a teaching job. It was generally expected of girls of my generation that they would work for a year or two until they found someone to marry, settled down and started a family. The expectations of and for women were similarly uninspired, most of the girls graduating from my school being given the choice of nursing, teaching, or 'something secretarial'. Had I studied science at school my choices might have been wider, but I had taken arts subjects — History, English and British Constitution — and my choice was correspondingly restricted. Until, that is, I discovered that I had the right qualifications to study law.

After attending an all girls school I couldn't wait to learn more about the opposite sex, so I applied to read law at university mostly because I knew that there would be more men than women in the Faculty of Law. Having chosen law for such a facile reason, I was surprised to discover that I had found my métier. I loved the interesting complexity of legal argument combined with the pragmatic simplicity of problem solving and so, after I obtained my degree, I went on to take the Solicitors' Qualifying Examinations and complete articles of clerkship (the equivalent of an apprenticeship). Finally, six years after commencing my degree, I was admitted as a Solicitor of the Supreme Court of Judicature. At the time this was an unusual career choice for a woman and I soon found that I was very definitely in a man's world. Personally, I found this exciting, although a little daunting. Most men were charming and encouraging but several treated me with dislike or disdain.

While I was completing my articles of clerkship, I met Ryan, a handsome, softly-spoken Australian, and we decided to marry immediately after I qualified. Our wedding was a typically pretty country affair followed by a working honeymoon in Australia. A year later we returned to England, intending to settle down and raise a family.

While scouting for an affordable house we came to Romney Marsh and fell in love with its wide open spaces and skies that stretched unbroken to the horizon. When we found Oldchurch, one of the ancient towns connected with the historic Cinque Ports, we were smitten with its tranquil character and its medieval houses all watched over by a towering church whose beauty had gained it the title of the Cathedral of the Marshes. At the end of the High Street we had discovered an old cottage was for sale. Although empty, it appealed to us and we made an offer for it the next day. A month later we were ensconced in a home of our own, with three bedrooms and a large garden. All that was lacking, until our children entered the world, was a dog. That vacancy was soon filled.

Poppadum was a border collie cross whose mother had refused to feed her. A friend came to see us for supper one evening and brought the tiny, fluffy puppy with him, snuggled under his coat. As soon as she emerged from her hiding place and staggered towards us, we were bewitched by her. Needless to say, she remained with us from that day onwards. She grew into a beautiful black, tan and white dog with a shining coat and limpid brown eyes that turned fierce if she thought either of us threatened. She was intelligent, quick to learn, affectionate and protective — what more could we have asked for in a pet?

Having found our home, the next requirement was employment. Ryan, who was a Chartered Accountant, took a position as company secretary with a firm in Ashford, while I settled for a full time job as an assistant solicitor with Messrs. Blackwater & Green, Solicitors and Commissioners for Oaths, in nearby Rye. Since we parted to go to work in opposite directions each morning, we had two cars. I owned an old Ford Anglia, a heavy monster of a vehicle. Generally reliable, it occasionally needed a push-start and, owing to the lack of hills in Oldchurch, usually required no less than five men to set their shoulders to it. Ryan was given a shiny new company car which was his pride and joy, but, in my opinion, it was not a patch on my Ford.

So there we were, happily installed in our first home, an enchanting cottage, with a job and a car each and a dog to share. All we needed to make our lives picture-postcard perfect was a child or two. And before long, I found I was pregnant. Our happiness was complete.

SOLICITING FROM HOME

At least, our happiness was complete until the dining room ceiling fell down and we discovered that the cottage had another inhabitant — death watch beetle. All the timbers of the old property had to be replaced. Not only did we have to face months of disruption, dust, dirt and builders on site, but we also had to find a large sum of money — much more than our savings — to pay for the building works. We had planned that I would give up work shortly before the baby was born so that I could be a stay at home wife and mother, but now it seemed impossible. We simply would not be able to manage financially.

Then one morning I had a brainwave. Why not apply for an overdraft to tide us over until the baby was old enough to leave with a baby-minder and I could practise law again? No sooner had I broached the subject with Ryan than he washed his hands of it. But I was made of sterner stuff. I felt sure I would be able to persuade Mr Standish, our bank manager, to give us a loan.

In the event that was precisely what happened. But, as I have already mentioned, Mr Standish also promised to help me to establish a legal practice in Oldchurch; support me by sending me clients; find me a baby-minder, a secretary, an office and anything else I might require. He was so delighted with the idea that he insisted on immediately telephoning a customer of the bank who was in need of a Will, because he was about to go into hospital for a serious operation. And before I knew it, an appointment was made and I was in business.

No wonder you could have knocked me down with a feather!

- 3 -

There was a timid tap on the front door. Poppadum merely raised a fawn eyebrow. I peeped out of the window. The view was obscured by the rampant yellow rose but I could see a pair of sensible ladies' shoes.

Rat-a-tat-tat. A sharper series of insistent raps followed. Someone else must have grabbed the knocker. Poppadum's ears perked up the instant before she threw herself at the sitting room door, barking wildly. I grabbed her collar and dragged her away.

"Quiet!" I bellowed. She obeyed reluctantly, grumbling. "Sit! Stay there."

She slid to the floor, keeping her eyes on me as I raced to the front door and threw it wide. An elderly couple stood there hand-in-hand, looking slightly nervous.

"Good morning," I said, with my best welcoming smile.

"Good morning," the gentleman greeted me, raising his hat. "Mrs Russell?"

Poppadum and I replied together — she with a conversational growl from behind the door and me with a "Yes." I ignored the growl. "What can I do for you?"

"Mr Standish said yer a solicitor. And that you'd make a Will fer us, quick-like."

"Oh! You must be Mr and Mrs White?" He nodded. "Mr Standish did mention it, but I thought he'd arranged an appointment for tomorrow. Please, do come in."

Mr White realised I was flustered by their arrival. "I'm sure 'e said this morning ter us. But no matter: we can come back."

"No, no. It's quite all right," I said, thinking of the pile of dishes in the sink waiting to be washed, and the disarray in the sitting room where I had begun polishing the furniture. Thank God I hadn't changed out of my formal clothes since visiting the bank manager, and at least I'd managed to dust and vacuum the dining room.

I backed into the dining room feeling Poppadum fuming behind the other door. I mentally warned her, on pain of certain death, not to make another sound. The thought must have reached her; I heard a long sigh and a thump as she lay down.

Mr White glanced at his diminutive wife. "Yer seem to 'ave a very big dog, Mrs Russell. My wife is not fond of dogs. 'E won't come near, will 'e?"

I realised that they were so nervous that they would run back up the High Street at the slightest provocation. I suspected that they were as scared of me — or at least of what I represented — as they were of the dog.

"No, no. I promise. I've shut her in the other room. Do come this way."

My smile returned, having slipped earlier without my permission. There was no answering smile from either of them. If anything, they looked even more uncertain as they followed me into the dining room.

'How do I put them at their ease?' I wondered.

I needn't have been concerned for my feet did it for me. As I turned to indicate a chair, I tripped over something and started tottering backwards. Mr White grabbed me instinctively and, to my horror, I found my bulk, off balance, pulling him towards me.

Luckily the table stopped our backward progression — but I was halted before Mr White could stop himself and he cannoned into the hardness of the Bump and bounced backwards towards his wife. She held up her hands to ward him off. Fearing he might fall, I caught his arm. We stared at each other for a moment — and then he chuckled and I collapsed in helpless giggles. Mrs White was quivering; for one brief moment I wondered if she were about to collapse until I registered that she was shaking with silent laughter. None of us appeared any the worse for our encounter.

Still overcome with amusement, I could only speak in short bursts:

"What … a way … for a … solicitor … to greet … her first clients!" I stuttered, "Please forgive me."

"Mr Standish did say as yer was a most unusual solicitor," chuckled Mr White.

"Yes, and 'e sed we'd find yer very friendly!" added his wife with a broad smile that showed the white perfection of her false teeth.

In the sitting room, Poppadum sneezed.

"Maybe we should all sit down now?" I suggested when I had regained my breath. Laughter threatened to break out again at any moment so I picked up a pad of paper from the desk, sat down in the carver chair at the end of the table and unscrewed the lid of my fountain pen, struggling all the while to compose myself. Still smiling, Mr and Mrs White sat side by side on my left. I noticed that they were holding hands again.

"Thank yer for seein' us so quickly, dear," said Mrs White.

"My pleasure, Mrs White," I replied. "As you can see,

SOLICITING FROM HOME

I'm having a baby next month and I'd planned to give up work for a while, but Mr Standish is very persuasive."

I was also very glad that I hadn't taken Myles' advice to drive back to the office in Rye. Instead, I had come home and started tidying up. I had also telephoned the senior partner at Blackwater & Green, but I already knew what his response would be because he had himself been encouraging me to take some time off before the baby's birth. He had chuckled at my account of Mr Standish's persuasiveness and told me to stay at home for the rest of the day.

Mr and Mrs White were looking bewildered.

"And I'm very glad to meet you," I continued quickly, smiling from one to the other. "So let's get started. I gather that neither of you has an existing Will?"

"Nope," responded Mr White. "I'm still not keen. Seems ter me that as soon as yer makes a Will, yer dies."

I steeled myself not to sigh. That old chestnut. It was always the same: people thought that making a Will was the equivalent of signing their death warrant, or perhaps they were so afraid of death that they simply ignored its inevitability. Either way, they ignored the importance of making a Will while they were of sound mind and healthy, and this nearly always led to problems — and sometimes conflict — for their nearest and dearest.

Mrs White appeared to be less vexed than her spouse.

"Now, now, dear. Yer knows we 'ave ter realise we'll die some time," she admonished. "Not terday, not termorrer, nor even next year, p'rhaps — but I'm sure Mr Standish's right ter send us ter Mrs Russell. If we does it now, it'll be one less thing ter worry about." She looked at me unswervingly as she continued: "Mr Standish speaks 'ighly of yer, me duck. 'E said yer'd 'elp us organise this very quick. It's urgent, see, 'cos my 'usband 'as ter go into 'ospital the day after termorrer. It's 'is prostrate, yer see."

"I see." I said, smiling inwardly at the mispronunciation. "In that case it would be best to get the Will made quickly, I think. Then there will be one less thing for you to have on your mind."

I turned my attention to Mr White, noticing his sallow complexion and obvious anxiety. His hands were trembling and it was clear he was in severe discomfort. My heart went out to them both.

"First, I need to check one thing. Are you *sure* that *neither* of you has *ever* made a Will before?" I asked.

"No," was Mrs White's swift response. She appeared to have recovered from her apprehension about Poppadum and now demonstrated an indefinable air of being able to cope with anything life threw at her.

"Long ago, in the Army," said Mr White, looking self-conscious. "Before I'd even met Phyllis."

"Did yer?" Phyllis White was amazed. "Yer never told *me* that. Well, I never!"

"I imagine it wouldn't be valid now," I said brightly. "Marriage annuls a Will, so it would be void anyway."

Mrs White's cheeks reddened alarmingly and a saucy smile reached Mr White's eyes, making them twinkle. I closed my eyes at the thought that I'd made such an obvious faux pas.

"Oh, I see … I've made a mistake." They weren't married. How could I have been so indelicate? How could I rescue the situation? I rushed on: "In that case, it may be even more important to make a Will now. Have you been together long?"

"Forty two and a bit years!" exclaimed Mrs White, her blush receding as quickly as it came. "Long enough. Eh, Archie?"

"Indeed! Congratulations," I responded, thinking fast but silently: 'Mrs White will have no automatic entitlement to any part of Mr White's Estate since she is not his wife: she will, at best, only have a claim. I suppose there's a distinct possibility that the Will Mr White made in the Army is still valid? At least it will be if he made it when he was on active duty, even if it wasn't correctly witnessed.'

I came to the swift conclusion that the sooner they made their Wills the better. I could make sure any previous Will was revoked and that new ones reflected their wishes and were executed properly.

"Tell me what you would like in your Wills," I pressed.

"Well, we ain't got much," said Phyllis. "I've made a list ov things. 'Ere."

She drew a slightly grubby piece of paper from her handbag and handed it to me. Mr White raised an eyebrow at Phyllis and put his hand in his pocket. He drew out a recent bank statement.

"That's what I've got," he said. "And I've marked what I want ter go ter 'oo."

I looked at the two pieces of paper. They represented two very different things. Phyllis' showed the contents of their house and two small savings accounts, one with the Post Office and the other with the Hastings and Thanet Building Society. On the other hand, Archie's statement showed a large five-figure sum invested through the bank.

Melanie Russell

A swift mental calculation of the considerable assets in Mr White's Estate, showed that Estate Duty would be payable and, since she wasn't married to Mr White, Phyllis had very little protection under the law. Unless....

"It seems that all these savings and investments are in your sole name, Mr White. Are any of them held in joint names?"

He shook his head. "Phyllis never wanted ter know 'bout that sort of thing. Wonderful manager, she is. I give 'er me pay-packet and she gives me back enough for a flutter on the 'orses. That's where that's all come from. Couldn't tell 'er I won, could I? She wouldn't 'ave let me 'ave me pocket money."

"So all this is your winnings?" I was astonished.

"Yes. Thought I 'ad all the luck. Steady job, winnin' on the 'orses, nice 'ome, Phyllis, children and then this flippin' — begging yer pardon! — cancer come from nowhere." Mr White lapsed further into Kentish. "A little discomfort goin' — if yer knows what I mean — then it stops completely and they puts in a flippin' — begging yer pardon! — caffitter. Ooh what a relief that was — and two flippin' days later I'm flippin' 'avin' a flippin' operation. It's a bloody flippin' nuisance, when all's said and done!" His sallow cheeks had reddened considerably in the course of this speech.

"I'm very sorry ..." I began.

"I've written down there all that I 'ave and 'oo I want ter 'ave it." He cast a wary look a Phyllis, who had been peering at the statement on the desk in front of me.

"Give it ter me!" She shouted as she grabbed the much-folded piece of paper from the table. "Yer never, ever told me 'bout this, neither! Look, *thirty thousand* pounds! We

SOLICITING FROM HOME

could 'ave bought our own 'ouse, we could 'ave ..." And, much to my concern, she burst into raucous sobs. "Oh, 'ow could yer, 'ow *could* yer ... yer knows 'ow much ... An' after all I've done fer yer ..."

I handed her the box of tissues I kept on the bookshelf. She pulled out a handful and blew her nose noisily.

Archie sighed, but his voice grew stronger. "I knew it — now yer'll go on and on 'bout 'ow much yer've done fer me."

This was too much for Phyllis.

"So I 'ave, yer ungrateful bastard! *And* 'ad 8 children of yours — not to mention that skinny lad yer got on Deirdre what she don't look after properly and as stays with us — *and* brought 'em up on next to nothin', *and* made all their clothes, *and* done cleaning for Mrs Jupp *and* gone fruit pickin', potato pickin' and every other sorta pickin'! Worked my fingers ter the bone, I 'ave, and *never* asked fer *nothin*! And all the while yer've bin saltin' away this and puttin' away that and, I expect *havin'* it away with ... OW!" she ended sharply. "What'd yer do that for?"

Her husband must have kicked her under the table, for she bent down to rub her leg. Okay, I thought, that's loosened the emotions, now it's back to me.

"You've obviously had quite a shock, Mrs White," I soothed. "I think a cup of tea would be a good idea. Do you take milk and sugar?"

"Milk with two sugars, please — an' the same fer 'im." She jerked her thumb at Archie.

I retreated to the kitchen, leaving them to sort things out between themselves. Fortunately, I had been about to make a cup of tea for myself when Mr and Mrs White arrived so the kettle was still warm. I set it on the hotplate and replaced the whistle, hoping that its screech would give my clients time to compose themselves before I sailed in with the tea.

The phone rang. I caught it to my ear immediately.

"Hello Mrs Russell. Good morning, Melanie!" Unmistakably Mr Standish. "I need to have a word about Mr and Mrs White."

"Too late, Mr Standish! They're with me now."

"I thought you should know that they're not actually married." He hesitated.

"I've discovered that, Mr Standish," I said drily.

"Has Mr White given you details of his investments with the bank?"

"Indeed he has."

"Oh, so you know?"

"Yes, I think I have all the information I need for the moment, thank you." The kettle emitted a shrill whistle. "I'm about to make them a cup of tea. Sorry, but I must go. Goodbye."

I flung the receiver down, rushed to lift the kettle from the heat but took my time making the tea. I rattled the cups as I left them by the hatch and when I re-entered the room my clients were quiet again. Archie had his arm round Phyllis and she was looking at him lovingly, her eyes still wet. It was a poignant scene. I cleared my throat.

'It's all right, dear," Phyllis said, smiling at me, seemingly back to her previous self. "Archie and me've decided as we've bin together too long now ter argue over things like 'oo 'as the money. At least 'e saved it. Anyone else would 'ave put it back on the 'orses and blown it all!" She smiled at Archie, an affectionate, slightly sad smile.

SOLICITING FROM HOME

"We've just got ter get on with gettin' 'im better so we can enjoy it. 'E ain't goin' ter get away from me now."

Archie squeezed her shoulder and took his arm away. He looked distinctly drained and more than a little grey, but he grinned roguishly at me as I handed him his tea.

"Life in the old dog, yet!" he crowed. "Let's get on wiv it, so's I can go 'ome and get to bed."

"I do advise you to make a more complicated, more tax-efficient Will when you're feeling better," I said, trying to be tactful. "I suggest you make a very simple Will for the moment. So I only need to know what…"

"Well, I wants Phyllis ter 'ave it all, a course." Archie interrupted. "*No-one* could've looked after me better — even if she do 'ave a naggin' tongue in 'er head and a vicious swipe wiv a tea towel!"

"Only when I 'ave ter, my man!"

"And Mrs White? Who do you want to leave it to?"

"But *I* ain't got no money, 'ave I?" She was smiling at me in a rather tolerant fashion as if I were simple. Oh dear!

"Not much at the moment, certainly; but — if Archie dies first — who would you want to have the money then?"

"Well, first, he ain't goin' ter die. And next, I wouldn't flippin' care would I? Not if Archie was dead."

I discarded the idea of trying to explain anything about the more complicated part of making a Will. A simple Will would suffice. Any outstanding matters could be dealt with after Archie's operation. I had to be pragmatic. If he died soon it would be necessary to make another Will for Phyllis anyway, since she would have inherited a great deal of money. There might be some Estate Duty payable on his death but that was a comparatively small consideration since Phyllis would inherit much more than she had expected earlier in the day.

"I want ter make sure Phyllis and the children are orl right if I ... don't make it." Mr White said, making it easy for me.

I had seated myself back at the table, my hands naturally forming a steeple on which I rested my chin, a hackneyed lawyer's attitude, I knew, but it always assisted my thinking process.

"Very well, this is what I advise," I said, with as much authority as I could muster. "I will make a simple Will for each of you in which you each leave everything to the other and then, when the second one of you passes away, to your children — including Deirdre's son, I presume? Is that all right with you so far?"

They glanced at each other and then chirruped "yes" in unison.

"You will need an executor. I expect you know that an executor is someone who carries out the legal side of dealing with the Estate?" They both looked at me blankly. "That's all the money and property you leave." I explained, hoping I was not lapsing into too much legal jargon. "It can be the same person who benefits under the Will, or someone else whom you trust. In fact, since you already have an account there, you might like to consider the bank as an executor. "

"Oh yes. Do yer think Mr Standish would?" Mr White seized on this suggestion. Phyllis nodded.

"I'm afraid it wouldn't be Mr Standish," I interjected. "The bank has a whole department to deal with such things. They are very efficient but sometimes rather impersonal — and can be quite expensive."

SOLICITING FROM HOME

"Would *yer*?"

I was in a fix here. I knew that the bank expected each of its managers to fulfil a quota of Wills in which the bank was appointed as the executor. Although he had not said so, I knew Mr Standish had recommended me to the Whites on the implied understanding that I would help him reach his quota. Most solicitors saw Wills as a future source of earnings and often recommended their own services. At least I did not have that consideration: I was merely drawing up some Wills to make a little money before the baby came. I had no intention of building a firm that would last for generations and, on a personal level, I wanted to help this engaging couple.

"I *could*, but I suggest that it would be simplest if each of you were to appoint the other as your executor. Then, when the time comes, you can take the Will to Mr Standish, or *any* solicitor you like, to help you with the Probate … the winding up of the Estate…" Four eyes surveyed me blankly. I tried to elucidate. "When someone dies there is a lot to do. Most people worry about the funeral and believe the rest takes care of itself. But there is much more to it than that, unfortunately. The executor has to give a sworn account to the Inland Revenue, called an Inland Revenue Affidavit. It lists the value of all the assets … things they owned … that were in the name of the deceased … I mean the person who has died. The Affidavit is sent to the Court of Probate, with another document that the executor has to swear, before what is called a Grant of Probate is given to …"

"I'd no idea it were so complicated, duck," interjected Mrs White, looking flummoxed.

"Mr Standish'll do it all," said Mr White. "Put '*im* down,

Mrs Russell, or the bank, fer the ex... ex... ex..."

"Very well," I said, saving him. I made a note to talk about executors again at another time. "I'll draw up two very simple Wills. In them, you'll each leave everything you own to the other and then on to your children — and appoint the bank as executor. Are you happy with that?"

"Yes, thank yer, Mrs Russell. And can yer make it so we can understand it, please? None of that lawyer-speak?"

I bit my tongue. Contrary to common belief, solicitors did not choose to write in riddles and were not paid by the word. As a result of legal cases too numerous to mention, the Court itself had decided what terminology and wording was most efficacious for conveying the right meaning.

"I'll do my best, Mr White. However, when you appoint the bank as executor there is a set clause that I have to use. Now, it's most important that your Wills are signed before you go into hospital. Would you like me to bring them to you tomorrow?"

"Er ... yes." Mrs White nodded.

"You will need two witnesses to be present," I continued. "I can be one but perhaps you would ask a neighbour to be the second witness?"

Mrs White thought for a moment, frowning, and then her face cleared. "I'll do it fer Archie an' 'e'll do it fer me," she declared.

"No, I'm afraid you can't," I said, shaking my head. "You see, if you witness a Will you can't take any of the money left to you by it."

They looked at each other, and then back at me, apparently mystified. I hurried to explain: "It's a safeguard to make sure that no one forces someone else to make a Will,

SOLICITING FROM HOME

or forges their signature," I explained. "The two witnesses have to be independent, adult and preferably not relatives of the person making the Will."

"All right," said Phyllis, still looking a little perplexed.

After a good deal of hand shaking and many thank-yers, they left, having agreed that I would call at their house the following morning. I breathed a sigh of relief, released Poppadum from her incarceration in the sitting room, and took my cup of cold tea into the summer-scented garden. I needed a breath of air before I sat down to type up their Wills.

Some hours later, I ripped a sheet of paper from the typewriter, screwed it up and threw it on the floor in a fit of pique. Poppadum jumped and let out a surprised 'woof'.

"You may well woof," I told her, my hands still shaking. "I wish I could bark, too. That's the fourth piece of paper wasted. I wasn't made to be a typist. Damn!" I buried my head in my hands, feeling tears of frustration trickle through my fingers.

"Damn and damn again!"

The muffled expletive was more of a sob than an exclamation. Who was this silly over-emotional woman? Well, obviously, it was me. Poppadum nudged me with her nose and then put her head in my lap. I peeked between my fingers and saw her looking up at me. It made me laugh. I caressed her soft fur with my fingertips.

"Thank you, sweetie-pie," I said out loud. "What would I do without you?"

It was not at all what I had been feeling about my canine companion a few hours earlier when she'd barked at the postman and attacked each letter as it was pushed through the letterbox. My mail was not fit to be filed — her teeth had penetrated every sheet. Nor had she been popular when I'd had to shut her in the sitting room because she had frightened Mr and Mrs White.

I was sitting at the table that I'd positioned so that I could look through the bedroom window eastwards towards the church. On it I'd placed a filing tray and the small portable manual typewriter my brother had given me when he had emigrated to Australia a couple of years previously. The typewriter had been second-hand when he acquired it, on the basis that it would be used only for typing the odd invoice or letter. The "s" key stuck very easily and the ribbon was hard to acquire and even more difficult to fit. I'd struggled to put in a new ribbon that afternoon before endeavouring to type the Wills for Mr and Mrs White.

It had not gone well.

The front door slammed and Ryan yelled: "Hello? Melanie? Where are you?"

"Darling, I'm up here — very hot and bothered."

I heard a thud as Ryan dropped his briefcase. Leaping up the stairs two at a time, he swept me into his arms and held me as close as he could, baby permitting. I felt better instantly.

"I love you being here when I come home," he said into my hair. He took a deep breath. "Your hair smells lovely even if you *are* hot and bothered. I know why you're hot but why are you bothered?"

The baby kicked him and he moved away with a rueful smile.

"These stupid Wills. See — I've drafted them here in

SOLICITING FROM HOME

biro." I showed him the lined pad with my close-packed writing on it. Several crossings out and amendments showed where I'd wrestled with the wording. "I've been trying to engross them all afternoon."

"Engross?" he queried, frowning in puzzlement.

"You know. Legalese for 'fair copy ready for signature'."

"Trying to? What's difficult? Has the typewriter been playing up?" He loosened his already loose tie and, after pulling it off over his head, he started undoing his shirt.

"No ... not really ... apart from that stupid sticky 's' ... No, it's me! I know I *started* to learn to type but I've never had to do it properly because I've always had a secretary. Now I have to engross Wills on this special paper. Look."

I held out a piece of the heavy, blue-grey paper. He threw his shirt on the bed and took the Will engrossment paper from me.

"I can see it's thick. Why is it doubled over?"

"It's special *Will* paper. See — the front has 'This is the Last Will and Testament' printed on it." I pointed to the words printed in large mock-copperplate writing. "It's a huge sheet, folded into two, because you can't attach anything to a Will, even another page."

"Why not?"

"Because it would give rise to the legal presumption that the Testator intended to change the contents of his Will — so it would be invalidated so as to prevent any misrepresentation of the Testator's wishes."

Ryan was looking at me as though I were talking complete gobbledegook.

"Anyway," I pressed on. "I have to use this paper and I have to type down this page." I pointed to the front with the heading. "Then this one," I turned the page and indicated the page on the left of the crease. "Then this one." I ran my finger down the opposite page and turned it over. "And here on the back I have to put the name of the Testator and a space for the date when the Will is signed and witnessed."

"Ah," nodded Ryan. "Complicated then."

"No ... it should be simple! But if I make a mistake in the typing, the whole engrossment is ruined because a mistake may invalidate the Will."

"So what exactly is your problem?"

"*After* I've typed the whole first page *perfectly*, I keep messing up the second one. And the page creases when I turn it through that *horrid* machine. I don't think the typewriter likes the double thickness. And — worst of all! — I *have* to have *two* of them ready by tomorrow." I finished, my voice rising in a wail.

Ryan had stripped to his underpants. "*Poor* Melanie," he cooed as he made for the door. "I need a cool bath now. I'll mull it over in there and see if I can find a solution. But I warn you — I don't mull well when I'm hungry!"

"Mull? Hungry? I'll ... I'll ..." I gave up trying to think of a threat and threw his clothes at him, but he jerked the door shut and escaped.

True to his word, Ryan did mull it over in the bath.

"You've already drafted the Wills. Suppose I read them to you? That would save you having to look up and down all the time. I expect you would even type more quickly."

I kissed his head as I handed him his plate of cold ham and salad. I was glad the weather was hot. We could exist on salad. No cooking required. But I'd baked some potatoes in their skins, thickly encrusted with salt, because Ryan didn't think a meal was a meal unless it included potatoes. I sat down and passed him the butter.

"That's a good idea. Maybe we could do it in the cool of the evening?"

I was watching him lavishly plonking butter on his potatoes as I wished I felt like eating; there was simply not enough room. I picked at a piece of ham. What I really wanted was a very large Mars bar.

"In the bedroom, eh? Great idea." He leered at me. I must have looked horrified because he grinned. "Don't worry, I know you won't be feeling like making love — but you have been warned. I shall be keeping a tally for afterwards."

"Being pregnant is not very sexy." I patted my belly. Much as I had loved being pregnant up to now, I was really feeling the heat and the lack of mobility. My ankles felt as if they were tree trunks. I looked down at them ruefully, sure they were swollen.

"You look wonderful to me, darlin'!" The response was a little slow in coming because he was ruminating on a large mouthful of buttery potato. The salad was looking a little forlorn; most of it was sitting on the side of his plate, uneaten. He gestured at my middle with his fork. "And if you're able to make a Will as well as a baby, you must *be* wonderful, too."

When the sun began its descent behind the willow tree, we made our way upstairs and settled down to work. Shadows crept along the wall and a cool breeze from the open windows fanned our cheeks. Unfortunately it had also ruffled my papers, most of which were strewn across the floor. Ryan picked them up and I shuffled them into order.

"I'll have to order some proper files," I remarked. "It's lucky I brought the Will paper home from the office. I did it only because I thought *we* needed new Wills now that we're going to be parents. The trouble is," I continued, "I've only got these four sheets left, so I daren't make any more mistakes."

"You won't," Ryan replied. "I'm here to help."

He settled me into a chair that was now a little too small for me. Gingerly, I inserted a doubled sheet of Will paper into the machine, turning the cylinder slowly. For once it came through perfectly, without a single crease down the fold.

My helpmeet picked up my draft and began to dictate: "'This is the Last Will and Testament'... you don't have to type that it's already printed ... 'of me Archibald Shakespeare Galsworthy Marlowe White' ..." He grinned. "What a name! 'of 5 Coronation Gardens, Oldchurch, Romney Marsh in the county of' .... Shouldn't there be a comma after 'me'?" he queried, looking over my shoulder.

"Nope." I continued to bash away at the typewriter. "There's no punctuation in Wills."

"Really?" He was most surprised, "Why ever not? How do you know how to read them?"

"Exactly. You can change the whole meaning of a passage with punctuation. There's a whole tranche of case law about the meaning of a comma in a certain place, so the convention is to use no punctuation at all."

"I can understand that bit I just read out," he commented, his eyes skipping down the page. "But what about this? '*I give, devise and bequeath*' ... do you *need* three words? ... 'my blah, blah, blah ... *unto and equally between* ...

SOLICITING FROM HOME

isn't that obvious? ... *my children* ... blah blah ... *provided they attain the age of twenty one years provided always that if any of them shall predecease me or not be proved to have so survived me leaving a child or children him or her surviving who shall attain the age of twenty one years such child or children shall take and if more than one equally between them the share or shares in my estate to which his her or their parent would have been entitled had he or she not so died as aforesaid.'*

He had run out of breath.

"Can you read a little more slowly?" I teased. "I can't type that fast!"

He smiled but not very deeply. "Honestly, Mel, I don't understand it. If I can't — and I'm *quite* clever — then how can anyone else?"

I sighed. I seemed to be sighing a lot recently.

"That's why it's best to go to a solicitor to make a Will," I explained patiently. "*We* understand it, you see! If I had the time I'd explain it — but for now, please pretend you're a tape recorder."

"Okay. Here goes. *'Whereby I revoke all former Wills'* — What is it, Melanie?"

I'd stopped typing and closed my eyes. Somewhat belatedly a thought had worked its way into my mind.

"I've just remembered that this is confidential and I haven't given you the confidentiality lecture or sworn you to silence."

Ryan looked amazed. "*What*? You *are* joking? I'm your husband."

"No. No, really I'm *not* joking. Everything between a solicitor and her client is confidential. We have to make this very clear to everyone in the office, from the cleaner to the cashier and *especially* to the secretaries. Now, unfortunately, you're not a tape recording machine so I will have to make you swear to keep this completely confidential. You are not to tell *anyone* anything about this, even in fun."

"Sure," he said. "I understand that, but you must admit that Archibald Shakespeare Galsworthy Marlowe White is a *most* amusing name."

"Please don't joke about it," I begged. "I'm deadly serious. I could be struck off the Roll of Solicitors if I divulged anything. I was taught not to recognise a client even if I passed them in the street — because they might not want anyone to know they'd been to see me. *Honestly*." I stressed the last word as I saw his face light up incredulously. "I can't even tell Mr Standish anything and he knows everything about Mr and Mrs White and even sent them to me."

"Okay, Mel, relax. I can see how important this is to you."

"Not to *me*," I interrupted. "To *my clients*. But of course it's important to me, too. I'm a member of a respected profession and I have to make sure that I keep that respect. *And* I have to keep the professional standards I swore to uphold when I was admitted. You remember, surely?"

He had been there when I was admitted as a Solicitor of The Supreme Court. We had been married only two days before the formal ceremony of Admittance. Kneeling with my hands clasped between those of the judge who administered it, I had sworn an oath that was as clear to me and as binding as my marriage vows. The formality and beauty of the ceremony had impressed Ryan who had added that he was very proud of my achievement.

SOLICITING FROM HOME

"*Of course* I remember and *of course* I won't divulge anything." He took my hands and replaced them on the typewriter keys. "Now, where were we? Oh yes, '*I give, devise and bequeath* ...*"*

It took over two hours but I eventually held two perfect Wills in my hands, one for Phyllis and one for Archie. I also had a somewhat bemused husband.

"If you're going to do more of this, I think you need some proper equipment," he said, hoarse from dictation. "Not only files, but a proper tape recorder with earphones and a foot peddle, and, I suppose, paper and typewriter ribbons."

"Next week," I agreed. "Or next month. But right now I need to stretch my legs."

The next morning, made up and in business mode, I walked slowly along Fleece Street, a quiet road that ran parallel to the High Street, to call on Mr and Mrs White. In my briefcase were their Wills for signature or, as we solicitors would say, 'execution'.

For most people, the term *execution* is inextricably linked with King Henry VIII's beheading of his wives, servants and allies. However, lawyers use it as a simple way of describing a process: 'to make valid by signing in the way required by the law'. As with many other legal procedures, there is a certain ritual to execution, rules that have to be obeyed to ensure that a Will is legally binding.

According to the law of England and Wales, no Will was valid unless it had been dated and signed by the testator (a word meaning 'any person who makes a Will') in the presence of two witnesses who were both adult (over eighteen years of age) and independent of the testator. I recalled that the Latin word 'testare' meaning 'to testify' was the root of the word 'testator'; the word 'testare' reflected the fact that, under Roman Law, a man swore an oath on his honour as a man, that is, on his manhood or, more precisely, on his testes.

I couldn't help grinning as my thoughts carried on in this vein. The legal term 'he died intestate' meant 'a man who died without having made a legally valid Will' — such a man must be lacking in two very important respects! — and a woman who died having made a Will was called a testatrix, despite never having had testes on which to swear.

I sobered as I remembered that when this part of the law developed it was legally impossible for a woman to own property, and thus only a man was able to dispose of his possessions by Will. In the case of married women, that had continued to be the case until the Married Women's Property Act was passed by Parliament in 1882.

My meditations on the singularity of English law came to an end as I approached the Whites' home in Fleece Row, off Fleece Street. It was in the centre of a row of terraced Victorian cottages built of red brick under black slate-tiled roofs. Phyllis opened the door, looking surprised to see me on the doorstep.

"Good morning, Mrs White," I greeted her. "I've brought your Wills for signature, as I promised."

"Oh! 'Mornin', Mrs Russell," she responded. "I was expectin' the doc, 'atcherly. Archie's not very well terday."

"I'm sorry to hear that. Is he well enough to see me, do you think? It's important that he signs his Will as soon as possible."

SOLICITING FROM HOME

"Yes, I 'spect he'll be the better fer it. Yer go up them stairs. 'Is room's straight ahead."

She moved aside to allow me access. I had put a foot on the first step of the staircase before I realised I had forgotten to check something.

"I hope I won't take long, Mrs White, I just need to read Archie's Will to him to make sure he understands it. I'm afraid there's no escaping some legal language and I may need to explain some of it to him," I said, grimacing a little. "The only problem is that I need another witness. I can be one, but…"

A loud knocking on the door made us both jump.

"…we need two," I ended limply as Phyllis opened the door. Doctor David Hadley stood on the doorstep, a battered medical bag in his hand. An older man of sixty five plus, hefty of build and grey of hair, he had been a well known rugby player in his youth. He was the senior partner in the local medical practice and over-due for retirement; but his wealth of experience and matter-of-fact bedside manner — sometimes matter-of-fact to the point of rudeness — were reassuring to the older inhabitants of Oldchurch.

"Good mornin', Doctor," Phyllis greeted him, a little obsequiously, bobbing as if she were about to drop him a curtesy.

"Good morning, Doctor Hadley," I echoed. He inclined his head curtly in reply, apparently expecting me to be leaving since it was plain that the tiny entrance hall was scarcely big enough to accommodate us all; however, he must have caught my last words.

"Two what?" he asked in his trademark brisk manner.

"Witnesses for Mr White's Will," I explained, equally briefly. "I can be one, but we need another."

"I presume I can do that for you," he said, the brief flicker that passed for a smile crossing his features. "But I must see my patient first. Lead on, Mrs White."

They ascended the stairs, Phyllis speaking in hushed tones to the doctor. I was left in the hall. 'Hall' was a very grand word for the tiny space at the bottom of the stairs, I thought, as I looked around for somewhere to sit. There was no chair, so I lowered myself onto the second stair and waited.

A few minutes passed. Then Dr. Hadley came out onto the landing above.

"You can come up now, Mrs Russell," he instructed peremptorily. "Mr White is ready to do the necessary."

I grabbed the Wills and took them upstairs, past the doctor and into the bedroom. Archie was sitting up in bed looking exhausted, but with a gleam in his eye which gave me hope that he would make a swift recovery from the operation scheduled for the morrow. I had a sneaking suspicion that it was pure funk which had sent him to his bed, partly from the fear of surgery but also from the superstition that making a Will was likely to kill him.

I showed him the Will, read it out to him and explained its terms in detail. I dwelt on the point that he would need to make a new Will if he married, even if he married Phyllis. I asked if he had any questions: he shut the eye nearest me in a wink.

"Not about the Will, duck. Leastwise, not now."

I handed Archie a clipboard and indicated where he

SOLICITING FROM HOME

should sign the Will. He did so laboriously, tongue poking out in concentration. Afterwards, I dated the document, witnessed it and proffered it to Dr. Hadley who did the same. Once executed, I folded the Will, put it carefully into its envelope and dated that too.

"Glad that's done, duck," said Archie from the bed. "Thank yer fer arrangin' it so quick like."

"A pleasure," I responded, inwardly amused remembering my fit of temper over the typing of it. "You make sure you hurry up and get well now — so I can make a longer and better Will for you." His eyes glinted so I forestalled him before he could make the inevitable comment. "Yes, and charge you the earth for it, of course!"

We bade each other farewell and the physician also took his leave. I shut the door firmly behind us feeling certain Archie was itching to get out of bed and into his clothes.

"Can you spare another minute or two to witness Phyllis' Will, please?" I said to the doctor.

He nodded terse agreement. Phyllis ushered us into the dining room, a poky space behind the small front room where I swiftly ran through the same formalities as I had with Archie, reminding her that the Will would be invalidated if she married. Three quick signatures and it was done.

Dr. Hadley bade us a brusque farewell and left. Before I departed, I reminded Phyllis that I would deposit the original Wills with the bank and send her copies of them. I would also keep a copy of each Will in case it were ever needed. Then, with suppressed excitement, I gave her an envelope containing the first bill I'd ever submitted in my own name.

As I was leaving, Phyllis laid her hand on my sleeve. "I want to thank yer for doin' this so quickly." She smiled, but there was a sadness in it. "'E may joke, but I knows it's bin worryin' Archie, not 'avin' a proper Will."

"He'll be fine now," I assured her. "The funny thing about making a Will is that it concentrates the mind on living."

For once, I was right. Mr White recovered well from his operation and a few weeks later I had the privilege of making fresh Wills for both of them. By that time, I'd had the presence of mind to write to them explaining the legal terms I would use. This made our conversation much easier, although much less amusing.

To my great pleasure, Mr White took Mr Standish's advice and made good, tax-efficient investments — the main one being to buy the house for which Phyllis had always longed. Best of all, Ryan and I were invited to their wedding and after an uproarious reception, to the ceremonial moment when Mr White, still in his formal suit, carried his bride over the threshold.

- 4 -

How can I describe my elation at the prospect of setting up in legal practice on my own account? It was so different from the joy of finding romantic love with Ryan: so dissimilar to the euphoria of knowing that he wanted to share his life with me and that of becoming his wife. The fun and delight of finding a home of our own was fulfilling and rewarding — especially since we had each other and our much-wanted dog to share it — but that was happiness rather than elation. And the excitement and joy of finding myself pregnant was different again since it contained a dash of fear and a pinch of future responsibility.

I suppose the main difference between all these joys was that those I've mentioned were shared, while the excitement of building up my own legal practice would be mine alone. I knew Ryan would support me, but I was the one who had the qualifications and knowledge that would make or break my firm. Even they were not enough in themselves. I would require perseverance, personality, a sense of humour, a sense of proportion and common sense. I would need to know how to negotiate all the hurdles of setting up a practice in the first place, and then to have the stamina and impetus to do what was necessary to promote the venture. Without clients, a practice would not survive and I could not rely solely on Mr Standish to provide them. I needed to make sure that people heard of me in a way that would encourage them to recommend me to others. Consequently I decided that there was only one way I would obtain those vital word-of-mouth recommendations — I would have to give an efficient, professional and personal service that was not obtainable elsewhere.

As I thought along these lines I realised, too, that my clients were likely to be people who had limited legal requirements for I was certain that the large, long-established local firms of solicitors would have mopped up all the landed and moneyed clients in the district. After all, I had worked for one of those firms, and I knew the loyalty of their clients to their 'personal' solicitor. I also knew that it was vital to stay on good terms with all the local solicitors' firms because I would need to be able to negotiate and communicate with them on behalf of my clients. For some time, I pondered over all these aspects of setting up in practice, wondering where my firm would fit into the grand scheme of things on Romney Marsh.

It was Mr Standish who came to my rescue. It had been agreed that I would take Mr and Mrs White's executed Wills to the bank for safe-keeping in the bank's vault. Concerned that the longer I kept them, the greater the possibility of something untoward happening to them, I took the Wills along as soon as they were executed. As it happened, Mr Standish was free when I appeared and he quickly ushered me into his office. I explained that I had made Wills that would cover the immediate situation and that I had suggested that Mr and Mrs White should consider making fresh ones when Mr White had recovered from his operation. "Mrs Russell, may I congratulate you?" He smiled at me, the effect magnified by the thickness of the lenses in his spectacles. "You prepared the Wills so quickly!

SOLICITING FROM HOME

And you typed them yourself?"

"Yes." I tried not to sound too pleased with myself, even though I was.

"Very good, my dear. Now, have you given any further thought to setting up a practice here in Oldchurch?"

"Yes, but ..."

"But?"

"I'm not sure how I could make it pay. How would I get clients to come to me? I know you have kindly offered to recommend me to your customers. But would that be enough? I'm not sure we have enough capital to buy the equipment necessary and it's one thing to type my own Wills but it's very labour-intensive and I could only work when the baby's sleeping." I stopped partly because I'd run out of breath and partly because Mr Standish was smiling. Actually, in the interest of accuracy, I have to admit that he was grinning.

"Mrs Russell, I have to say that I think you are too fearful. The bank will support you and you have already made your mark. You are able to show the human face of the law. Do not discount the value of that. Not only that, you have gone out of your way for Mr and Mrs White and I am sure you will do the same for any client. Do not discount the value of *that*, either. I think there's a strong possibility that you may find yourself too busy rather than not having enough to do!"

"Thank you for reassuring me."

"I can do more than that. I have many more Wills where those came from ... But I expect you would like a bit of a rest until your baby's born?"

"Er, yes. I think I need a chance to catch up on some

sleep."

"Too true! You won't get much afterwards. But maybe if something urgent comes up?"

"Of course."

I left feeling much happier than when I had arrived. Happy enough to allow my heart and spirit to soar with the idea of my own practice. Let Ryan pour cold water on the idea at his peril! I was on my way. Stop me if he dared.

Now I had the reassurance I needed there was nothing in my way. Although I'd never considered starting my own practice, now it was about to begin there was nothing I wanted more. Fancy being my own boss! Daunting it might be but how exhilarating, too.

'Oldchurch, here I come!' I exulted inwardly as a huge smile settled on my face.

Originally a small island amongst the tidal marshes, Oldchurch had first been inhabited by Stone Age people who had stopped to fish and forage. The Romans also lingered there, using the shallow lagoons and shingle banks around Oldchurch to make salt. After them, Danish Vikings had stopped to fish and stay for a while. But it was the Saxons who were the first to settle permanently on the island. It was they who had built the first church — the successor of which, centuries later, would rise far above the original Saxon building, its beautiful elegant façade and arched interior gaining it the title of Cathedral of the Marshes. The church, like most of the substantial properties that had been built by merchants, owed its existence, and its opulence, to the white gold that grew and grazed upon the marshes — sheep.

A wondrous and sometimes mysterious place where sky,

SOLICITING FROM HOME

land and sea meet in a glorious pageantry of colour, Romney Marsh stretches inland eight miles from the English Channel and fourteen miles along the coast from Hythe in Kent to Rye in Sussex. An area both exposed and isolated, it produced a hardy breed of sheep that had several advantages. These sheep had little interest in straying, thus requiring minimal fencing and little attention. They were good to eat, but above all they were valued for their wool. In truth, Romney Marsh sheep were a treasure that provided a good living for the Marsh folk. By the Middle Ages Romney wool was prized all over Europe, but this proved a burden rather than a benefit because in 1240 a heavy tax was levied on wool to finance England's many wars. The tax remained in place for hundreds of years with the result that the white gold was widely smuggled.

In the nineteenth century, Romney Marsh sheep were exported to New Zealand and Australia where they flourished and formed the basis for the wool and meat industries in those countries. But to those who lived in Oldchurch, through century after century, they were the basis for the wealth of the region, a source of both profit and pride.

Sea-faring was also an occupation that drew many a young man from the Marsh. Fishing and transporting goods were legal trades, but, with their knowledge of the coast and tides, many a fisherman became a smuggler or a pirate in times of hunger, or when adventure beckoned. The Crown found a way to make use of these skills: in 1155 a Royal Charter established the Cinque Ports Confederation, under which five ports — Dover, Sandwich, Hythe, New Romney and Hastings — were required to maintain ships ready for the defence of the Realm and in return were given important rights and privileges. The Ports' duties were shared by seven 'Limbs' and two Ancient Towns. Oldchurch was appointed a 'Limb' of the Cinque Port of Romney, while Rye, one of the 'Ancient Towns', later became a full member of the Confederation.

But that was history. I thought warmly of the more recent past: how well I remembered the Christmas Eve, only eighteen months previously, when I had first driven Ryan towards the Marsh.

On a chilly, damp morning, the sun had been struggling to throw off its night-time eiderdown of cloud as we left my parents' house and drove through narrow lanes winding between high, bare hedgerows. Here and there a copse of trees stretched their branches towards the sky, the rooks' nests in them making a pattern like inkblots on blotting paper. At the top of the cliff that forms the escarpment along the inland edge of the Marsh, marking the old shoreline of Saxon days, we seemed, for a moment, to be suspended in space. A broad expanse of flat land stretched before us as far as the eye could see, patch-worked with shimmering, sparkling hedges awash in a soft pink mist that merged into a sky of pale, pale blue. I drove carefully along the narrow road which looped down the steep hillside, braking hard on the corners to slow our descent.

A blush of mist greeted us. Shimmering droplets clung to the boughs of the willow trees which leaned over the dykes, droplets which caught the light from the low sun and sparkled rose-pink in the gentle light. The dykes twisted with every turn of the narrow road, thin rivers of mercury

SOLICITING FROM HOME

lined with silver speared rushes.

I had pulled up and turned off the engine and the magic of the English countryside in winter flung its spell over us. All was quiet; for once, there was no traffic. A watery sun fingered the occasional tall, bare tree and a distant church spire rising ghostlike from the haze. We drank in the transient beauty of the Marsh in hushed appreciation. For me, that moment still stretched into infinity.

Neither of us had spoken when I re-started the car and drove slowly on, the road uncoiling before us through acres of flat marshland, the reed-tangled dykes our constant companions.

That had been in winter: summer brought a softer prospect. Only yesterday, in late May, I had driven along the narrow lanes that lead from Oldchurch to Rye, snaking through the southernmost stretch of the Marsh where the shingle beach edges the fertile marshland. In winter, when cold winds swept in from the sea, it resembled a barren wilderness, windswept and bleak, but now that it was early summer the land had decked itself in wild flowers. The gentle breeze set them dancing, their radiant petals bright against the green grass shimmering in the sunshine. It whispered on amongst the darker green of the reeds that edged dykes and old shingle quarries alike, the latter now flooded to become shining lakes of deep gentian blue, a perfect reflection of the cloudless summer sky mirrored upon their still surfaces.

And then there had been that wonderful moment in early April, not long after we had moved into Rose Cottage, when I had woken one night feeling warm and contented, infused with gratitude for all that my life held. Moonlight flooded the room and a gentle breeze stirred the curtains: I crept to the casement and looked out into the garden. Truly it was a night made for dreaming contemplation — a white night, full of the moon and the magic of the moon. She peeped down at me through the whispering new leaves of the willow and apple trees, chequering the shadows with silver and turning the stream at the bottom of the garden into a path of pewter fit for the feet of fairies. As I stood staring at the moon's pale loveliness, I inhaled the perfume of flowers, herbs and the dewy earth, while from the mysteries of the little wood beyond the brook stole the soft, sweet song of a nightingale.

And now, wanting to stretch out this time of internal contemplation, I decided to take the long way home across the fields. Above the verdant pastures, dotted with sheep but uncluttered by buildings and trees, the swirl of wind currents painted ever-changing cloudscapes in the sky; sun and shadows reflected across flat meadows of green divided by still, dark dykes edged with rushes and the lace of cow parsley. A small lamb's fleece of cloud floated across the face of the sun, catching golden crumbs within its wool. Finger-beams of light fanned out in blessing upon the land beneath for the space of several heartbeats — until the breeze exhaled a long slow breath, disentangling the golden fleece which floated onwards. The sun's face, unveiled, struck filaments of gold and slivers of silver from the surface of the dykes and a kingfisher flashed into the water and away, its back glistening electric blue light. My senses revelled in the light; the freshness of the air with its under-scent of sheep; the lush softness of the grass beneath my feet combined with

SOLICITING FROM HOME

the warmth of the sun on my hair; but above all, the lack of mechanical sounds — there was only the gentle rustling of the breeze in leaves and rushes, the occasional bleat of a sheep and the hum of the insects on which sparrows feasted. I closed my eyes and drew in a deep breath, tasting the freshness of the air on my tongue. I wished only to keep this feeling of harmony with Nature within me forever.

My heart lifted. I opened my eyes and came back to the present.

Yes! Oldchurch was the perfect place to start the type of business I had in mind. A small but ancient town in a unique landscape. Indeed, it was Oldchurch's situation that made it, for me, incomparable. Set in the centre of Romney Marsh, it might not be an obvious place to set up a solicitor's practice. For most people, its isolation would make it unattractive; but it boasted a population of some four thousand and more people lived in the surrounding villages. New Romney, the Cinque Port of which Oldchurch formed a Limb, was only three miles distant and, although the two towns were traditionally at daggers drawn, there was no solicitor's practice there, either. Although I knew that many people would already have a firm of solicitors who acted for them, there would be others for whom the convenience of a local office would be both an attraction and a benefit.

But the most delightful thing of all was that I would not have to travel. I would be able to both live and work in this beautiful town in a landscape I loved, where there was a community of people who treated each other as individuals and not as numbers. My heart belonged to the Marsh and the people who lived there. Among them would be the new life that I would be bringing into the world. My baby would be able to breathe and laugh and run freely in this special part of the world.

The thought made me smile as I recollected that Ford Maddox Ford offered these words as a quotation in his book on the Cinque Ports : 'these be the five quarters of the world, Europe, Asia, Africa, America and the Romney Marsh.' Kipling later added 'Australy' to the list, and thus Romney Marsh had become known to all and sundry as 'the Sixth Continent'.

Not many solicitors could draw their clients from a whole continent!

- 5 -

"Good God! What's that?" I exclaimed, startled by a thunderous thumping on the front door.

I had just come in from walking Poppadum. Her lead was still in my hand as I rushed to open the door before it was shattered, Poppadum growling behind me. A stout, grey-haired lady nearly fell into my arms. She was very flustered, almost shouting, talking fast and furiously. Poppadum started barking.

"I must see the solicitor. At once! It's *most* urgent! Very urgent! I must see him *now*! Tell him *at once!*"

She waved her hands, her voice crescendoing to a bellow as she endeavoured to make herself heard over Poppadum's fury.

"*At once! Mrs Kendall*. My name is *Mrs Kendall!*"

So far my efforts to quieten Poppadum had proved utterly ineffectual, Mrs Kendall's flapping arms serving only to inflame the dog's need to protect me. Catching a glimpse of teeth bared in a ferocious snarl, I grabbed Poppadum by the collar, stroked her gently and whispered to her. "It's all right, Old Girl, quiet now."

Poppadum grumbled, but quietened. I addressed Mrs Kendall: "Do come in and have a seat ..." I began soothingly, still holding the dog's collar.

"*No! No*. I can't sit down. I told you. *It's urgent!*" she boomed, so close to my ear that I actually flinched. "I *must* see him at once!"

Poppadum made a distinctly threatening noise somewhere between a growl and a bark.

"Shush!" I admonished her, as she eyed Mrs Kendall speculatively. The latter had followed me into the sitting room. Slightly deaf in my right ear, I motioned her to an armchair.

"Please tell me ..." I tried again.

"No, I can't tell *you*. I *have* to speak to the *so-li-ci-tor*," she said, spelling it out for me. "My business is *private* and *urgent*."

She was becoming so agitated that I feared that she might have a stroke and drop dead on the spot. I raised my voice.

"I *am* the *so-li-ci-tor*! Now, Mrs Kendall, *please* take a seat and I'll be with you in a minute."

She looked at me curiously for a moment and then dropped into the armchair like a stone.

"Would you like a cup of coffee or a glass of water?" I asked, heading for the kitchen with Poppadum.

"No. No, thank you." Her voice had dropped a couple of octaves.

I hung up Poppadum's lead and settled her in her basket, commanding her to stay there and to stay quiet. She showed her disapproval by turning round and round before she lay down with her back to me, but with a wary eye on Mrs Kendall. I filled two glasses with water, placing them through the hatch into the dining room. When I returned to the sitting room Mrs Kendall was sitting straight-backed in one of the armchairs, looking uncomfortable.

"Sorry about the noise, Mrs Kendall. Poppadum is very

SOLICITING FROM HOME

protective of me at the moment. Let's go through here into what serves as my office."

My new client heaved herself to her feet as I led the way into the dining room. I was grateful for my glass of water. My throat was parched and sipping it gave me time to collect my thoughts. Mrs Kendall accepted her glass from me absent-mindedly, taking a quick sip as she moved to the window, her eyes raking the street outside as if she were looking for someone.

I allowed myself a moment to survey her. A strand of her greying curly hair, escaping the neat French pleat, twisted around a beautiful complexion, though now rather hectic in colour. She turned and I found very bright blue eyes inspecting me.

She had been surprised that I was the solicitor. I presumed that she'd expected someone older and a man. I was as accustomed to this expectation as I was to the dismay and disappointment that often surfaced when the solicitor proved to be a young woman. I had recently applied to join the Kent Law Society, my application apparently causing some consternation among my fellow solicitors as the approval of my application took considerable time. It was made clear to me, in no uncertain fashion, that I was fortunate indeed that an older lady who practised near London had set a precedent — for it transpired that I was only the second lady solicitor to apply to become a member of that esteemed Society. I was aware that there were not many local solicitors and certainly very few who were women as young as I, let alone pregnant and living in a small town like Oldchurch.

I held out my hand. "Shall we start again? How do you

do, Mrs Kendall?" I smiled what I hoped was a reassuring smile. "My name is Melanie Russell. I've been qualified as a solicitor for a little over three years."

"How do you do, Mrs Russell?" she replied, shaking my hand firmly but briefly. "I am indeed sorry to have disturbed you, but something has occurred — it's most urgent."

She ensconced herself into a chair on the other side of the dining table while I wedged myself into the chair opposite her and invited her to continue.

Mrs Kendall was so wound up that she could not sit still: she fidgeted with the pen I had placed in front of me, her eyes following the movement of her fingers. After a long moment of silence she offered me the pen. I took it. She leaned forward and spoke in lowered tones:.

"I have a problem with my neighbours. I've known for a long time they've been trafficking Pakistanis into the country because I hear things at night. Footsteps, people shuffling around, whispers." I must have looked askance because she looked at me sideways, her well-modulated, cultured voice strengthening, as she continued: "Oh, they try to keep it quiet. But I've *heard* them. Often. Yes, very often. And sometimes I've seen them passing beneath my window. It's not easy to see them because they dress the poor creatures in black, and their skins are so dark. But I see the whites of their eyes. They are *so* afraid. Oh yes! They try to keep them quiet. *But I know.*"

"Mrs Kendall, are you s …" I was beginning to wonder whether she were a little deranged. She waved my interruption aside with an imperious hand and raised her voice.

SOLICITING FROM HOME

"*Of course* I'm sure. That was what you were going to ask, were you not? They all ask the same thing — everyone I dare to talk to. Even the police. Do you think I would come if I weren't?" she broke off, taking a deep breath, and I seized my chance.

"You've been to the police?" I asked.

"Yes, yes! I told them all I'm telling you. I've told them that Pakistanis are smuggled into the loft. I've told them that I hear noises in the night — muffled footsteps and shuffles. And sometimes a muffled cough or a cry ..."

Her voice died away as she fixed my eyes with hers. Her eyes were wide and her pupils dilated, very bright. She shook slightly. With a shock, I recognised her heightened mental state. 'Is she schizophrenic?' I thought in panic.

She had not stopped speaking. "... but no-one believes me. No-one will *do* anything. And I ... I have to admit ... I'm frightened. I don't like to admit that. I'm a proud woman, unlike some of these namby-pamby nitwits that live round here. But I *am* afraid. I'm sure I'm being followed," she divulged, her hands trembling.

"I'm sorry," I tried again, putting a hand over hers. She shook it off impatiently.

"I don't want sympathy!" she exclaimed angrily. "I'm trying to get you to *do* something. Let me spell this out to you as concisely as I am able. My next door neighbours bring in Pakistanis. How, or by what means I do *not* know. I only know they take them up into the attic ... into the loft which runs over my bedroom. I can't get up there — I have no access. How *they* get them up there I don't know either."

"But why do you think ...?" I started.

"Think? *Think*? I don't have to *think*! I *know*. I'm telling you! *Listen* to me. They keep them like *slaves* up there. Yes, just like the black slaves in the old sailing ship days. As a rule, they lie there, quiet. They are soon collected and taken away — to London, I expect," she swallowed, noisily. "But last week, someone *died* up there!"

This was too much for me. "But how do you know that?"

"There's a patch on my bedroom ceiling. I've watched it grow. It's the shape of a human form. And there's the smell. I know the smell of death when I smell it!"

"Er … Mrs Kendall …" I tried to forestall her, but she was in her stride now.

"I was a matron in a Singapore hospital in the War when the Japs overran it. Then I was a POW — a prisoner of war — for nearly four years. Oh, yes! I know the smell of death all right!"

"You were in Changi?" I was taken aback, thinking that what she must have suffered in a Japanese prisoner-of-war camp would be enough to unbalance anyone's mind.

"Indeed! But before that I ran the whole show at the Kerdang Kerbau hospital. That was in the days when nurses were *nurses*, not glorified air hostesses that just take temperatures and blood pressure. We used to deal with birth and death every day. They were all brought to my hospital, until Singapore was taken and then …. But what are you going to do about the Pakistanis?"

"You say you've told the police? This really is a criminal matter, not a civil one."

"Of course I've told the police. I've told you that

SOLICITING FROM HOME

already," she said heavily.

"What did they do?" I queried.

"Sent some young constable round to have a look. I told him all I knew — which is exactly what I'm telling you. All he did was to go and talk to the neighbours. I don't believe he went into the roof."

"Why not?"

"They must have spun him some tale. I expect the neighbours told him I was deranged and, no doubt, he believed them. I suppose I seem like a resentful old biddy." Her shoulders slumped, but her voice strengthened again. "But I know what I hear. *And* I know what I see. I hear the noises. I see the whites of their eyes. And I know what I smell, too — and it's the *smell of death*, I'm telling you." She paused and then went on more quietly: "I know you don't believe me. I know I sound deranged. But, believe me, I am *not* the fanciful sort, generally. This whole affair is very disconcerting and not a little frightening."

"Did the police report back to you?"

"Yes. They were not at all helpful. They said they'd investigated but had found no evidence of anything suspicious. But that was *before* the death. And the smell! I can't sleep in my own bedroom because the smell is so bad — with that big, dark shape on the ceiling made by all the body fluids."

"*If* there's been a murder, it's definitely a case for the police," I said firmly, in the hope of avoiding further comments about the smell of death. I was beginning to feel queasy.

"The police won't do anything. I told you, I tried. They

think I'm a time-waster. I'm resigned to it. Young people nowadays have no respect for their elders. But I know the neighbours have no right to use my loft space. Now that *is* a civil matter."

"Perhaps …" I began.

Snorting with annoyance, she jumped to her feet and cried distractedly, "No *'perhaps'*. I *must* do something. *You* must do *something*."

She was walking up and down the room. My eyes followed her as I tried to think of something to say, let alone do.

"I don't quite see what I can do."

"Just come round to my home. See the mark I'm talking about. *Smell* the *smell*! Talk to them. *Demand* to go up in the loft to inspect it. They must be made to stop this dreadful trade."

I was beginning to feel completely out of my depth. Never before had I been confronted by such a mentally-unbalanced woman in my office, let alone in my dining room. I had certainly never heard anyone mention 'the smell of death' before. This was a far cry from my usual round of Wills and Conveyancing which, although they could prove emotive on occasion, were matters that produced emotions with which I was used to dealing. Such apparent insanity was quite another thing.

"Please sit down, Mrs Kendall. I need to take a few details."

My firmness seemed to calm her and she reseated herself while I took down her name, address and telephone number and made a few notes of dates and times. The ordinariness

SOLICITING FROM HOME

of it calmed me as well.

"From what you've told me, Mrs Kendall, this is a criminal matter and should be reported to the police. Now I'm going to ring the police and I would like you to tell the constable exactly what you've told me."

"He won't beli ..."

"He will have to take it seriously if he knows I do. I'll accompany him to make sure he inspects the loft, and then I can see if I believe you have any civil claim against your neighbour. Are you happy with that?"

I began to feel in control of the situation again. Mrs Kendall felt it, too. "Yes. Very well, you may call the police. But I *will* require you to be present and to advise me. What will your fees be?"

"Shall we see if there's anything I can do, first? I'm not sure that I can help you. If I can't, I won't make a charge." It appeared generous, I hoped, but I didn't want to be retained by this strange woman unless there was something I could do to help — and unless there was some substance to her accusations.

"Thank you. How kind of you! Will you make that phone call now?"

"Yes, of course," I replied as I picked up the receiver and dialled the police house. Martin, the local constable, was not there but his wife said he would be back soon.

"I'd be very grateful if you would ask him to telephone me as soon as he returns. Thank you." I put the receiver back on its cradle with a click.

"He won't ring," Mrs Kendall prophesied. "They all think I'm out of my mind. But I really do know the smell ..."

"Yes, yes, Mrs Kendall," I interrupted hurriedly. "But I didn't mention you. And Martin always rings me back. There's not a lot I can do for you until I speak to him, so would you like to go home? I'll telephone as …"

"No!" she cried, leaping to her feet again and amazing me with the ease with which she moved her bulk so swiftly when I had such difficulty with my swollen belly. "No, I'll wait here. They saw me come out. They may have followed me here. And they've got a lot to hide. I'll wait here."

Mutely, I passed her glass of water to her. She might have been followed — goodness me, she was making me nervous now. We were sitting there, silently sizing each other up as we waited for the telephone to ring. When it did, only a couple of minutes later, we both jumped.

I answered it immediately.

"Hello Mrs Russell, I hear you need my help."

Martin was a young, fair-haired man who knew practically everyone in Oldchurch. I had not consulted him professionally before but I knew him reasonably well because we both served on the committee of the local youth club.

"Yes, Constable," I said, thinking it best to speak formally. "I have Mrs Kendall here. She has a problem and would be grateful for your help. She believes a crime has been committed."

"Not the Pakistanis again?" I could feel the sigh in his voice as I hesitated. "Surely, it can't be?"

"Yes, you are quite right, Officer," I confessed. "I wasn't involved before, but this time I think it may be serious."

His long sigh was audible to me: I hoped Mrs Kendall

SOLICITING FROM HOME

had not heard it. I pushed the receiver still closer to my ear.

"She's as nutty as a fruitcake," Martin declared. "I'll be with you as soon as I can." My heart sank at the thought of spending more time waiting.

"Within five minutes, do you think, Officer? Mrs Kendall is most anxious."

"I'll be there," he promised.

True to his word, Martin arrived five minutes and twenty-three seconds later and by that time I had managed to reassure Mrs Kendall that he would take her complaint seriously. I had ascertained that the deeds to her property were held at the bank and arranged that she would bring them to me so that I could check her legal title. I had also agreed to inspect the roof space on her behalf. I sincerely hoped that the neighbours would be available; to arrange another time might prove difficult and, in view of what Mrs Kendall had said, I wanted to inspect the property adjoining hers when the occupiers were unprepared for the visit.

Martin took off his helmet to enable him to walk through my low front door. Looking both handsome and friendly, he shook Mrs Kendall's hand.

"Mrs Kendall is concerned that her neighbours are using her roof space for illegal purposes," I informed him, retaining my formal manner. "She tells me that there is no access to the roof space from her property, although of course, she believes that she owns it. She's not sure what her neighbours are using it for, but she thinks it may be to cultivate drugs or to store stolen property. I suggested that she should contact you but she fears you may be of the opinion that she's wasting your time. I assured her that you would take this matter most seriously."

He nodded, giving me a speaking look. "Of course."

"I have also advised her that I should inspect the property and the deeds, so that I can make sure that the one relates to the other. If she owns the roof space to which she has no access, she may wish to take remedial steps." Gosh. I was sounding formal even to my own ears. I spoiled it by grinning. "So I thought we could assist each other by visiting it now."

"Right. Let's go." He headed out of the door, replacing his helmet once outside. His bicycle lay against the low wall.

"You go on ahead," I suggested. "I'll accompany Mrs Kendall. It's not far."

We walked the short distance to the house known as 'Old Owlers' in fairly companionable silence.

Ten minutes later Mrs Kendall and I rounded the corner into Draper's Road. Martin was talking to a youngish, pleasant-looking blonde woman who was standing on the steps of a wide old building that stood back from the road, separated by some distance from its neighbours. Surveying the building closely with my property lawyer's eye, I guessed that it was originally a 'hall house' and at least four hundred years old. Clearly, it had originally been built as a single dwelling; then later extended and subsequently divided into two smaller residences.

The woman turned towards us as we approached. I noticed that she was wearing heavy make-up, her foundation a touch too dark for her skin, her eyelids and eyelashes darkened too. She wore bright red lipstick.

"Hello, Mrs Kendall," she said before turning her

SOLICITING FROM HOME

charming smile on me. "You must be Mrs Russell. I'm Nancy Dean. Call me Nancy." She held out a red-nailed hand. "I'm sorry my husband isn't here. He's away on business. Martin tells me you would like to check the roof space for Mrs Kendall. That's fine. We've just cleared it out, so you timed it well."

She was still smiling; but there was something in that smile that was just a smidgeon too fulsome. For the first time, I wondered if there were any truth in Mrs Kendall's story. After brief greetings from my new client and myself, Nancy led the way up to the loft.

"It's true, you can only access the loft from our side of the house. I suppose it's a legacy from when it was all one house, before it was divided into two. I'm not sure when that was. Do you know, Kate?"

I was amazed that she addressed my client so familiarly; I would not have been comfortable doing so. Mrs Kendall had stressed that her Christian name was Catherine. She did not have the air of a 'Kate' at all.

"Actually, my name is Catherine," she corrected, plainly annoyed by the familiarity, and I was pleased that my judgement in this small thing was correct. "No, I have no idea. The property had been divided before I came here. As you know, that was over twenty-five years ago, not long after the War."

We had been climbing the stairs during this conversation and had now come to a crooked door on the second floor which opened onto a narrow, winding staircase, boarded on both sides, that led to the loft. I noticed a cupboard let into the side of the staircase wall, the sort that used to hold candles and candlesticks for those venturing upstairs. The stairs to the attic were steep and uneven, dimly lit by a single lightbulb. I had expected the loft to be similarly lit but when Nancy flipped the switch as we entered, artificial daylight flooded the place.

I noticed that it smelled stuffy and damp but that was all. No dead body nor any stain on the floor where it might have lain. Perhaps significantly, the whole area had been floored comparatively recently; it was also very clean. Nancy had mentioned that they had just cleared it — still, there was something a little odd about the place. Was I imagining it? Or was there a feeling that it had been vacated recently?

My eye caught a glint from the floor. I picked up a small piece of metal, shaped roughly like a doughnut, and handed it to Nancy. Now I was standing close to her, I noticed a livid bruise all down her left cheek that was just visible beneath her thick make-up. Her eyes narrowed as she took the object, her right eye closed more than her left and I noticed a flicker of pain. I guessed her eye-shadow hid a black eye. She took the object and moved quickly away from my scrutiny.

"Thank you," she said. "I wondered where I'd lost that button. I must have caught it on something when we were cleaning up here."

I was about to comment that there was not much to catch it on, and that it looked more like a washer than a button to me, but I thought better of it, and said instead: "Thank you for showing us up here, Nancy. Can you show me where the dividing line is between the two properties? Is it marked in any way? *Mrs Kendall* …" I stressed the surname "… needs more storage and is thinking of dividing off her half and

SOLICITING FROM HOME

making a separate access to it from her side."

"It would make it a much smaller space," Nancy observed. "I don't think it has ever been divided and I have no idea where the correct boundary would be. In fact I believe *we* own the flying freehold."

"That's interesting," I commented. "Mrs Kendall has instructed me to check her title deeds to her property, so I'll be able to ascertain the precise position. If she has legal title to half the loft and decides to go ahead with a division, I'm sure she'll instruct a surveyor to make sure there are no structural ramifications."

"At least she'll know there are no Pakistanis on *her* side then," she remarked.

Mrs Kendall bridled but said nothing. I watched Nancy closely; her fixed smile stuck to her lips as if glued in place, but she paled a little and the bruise became more apparent, despite the concealing cosmetics. Martin was ready to go.

"I think we've seen all there is to see. Is there anything else you want to check?" he asked.

A thought struck me. "Where do the pipes run, Nancy? Maybe the sound of running water is what disturbs Mrs Kendall."

Nancy looked away but not before I noticed that her smile had disappeared. "I really have no idea. There must be a tank somewhere, I suppose. I think it must be above our heads, up in the roof space. Where's your water tank, Catherine?"

"It's in the roof above the back extension," she answered stiffly.

"Time to go," I said. The stuffiness, heat and damp came

together in a noxious brew: my head whirled. I clutched the wooden bannister on the way down. Reeling into the sunlight, I had no option but to sit down abruptly on the doorstep. The whole street seemed to be spinning in a most peculiar way. Mrs Kendall took control.

"Melanie needs a chair. Quickly, Martin! And a glass of water, Nancy." To me she commanded, "Open your knees, my girl! Here, put your head down as far as you can."

I felt a slight pressure on my neck as my head came into contact with my smock and the baby took the opportunity to kick me on the chin. Whether it was pure embarrassment, or the chair, or the water, I have no notion, but when I raised my head the street came slowly into focus again. I took a deep breath and considered standing. Everything revolved fast and the world was blotted out by blackness.

When I came to, I found myself lying on an unfamiliar settee in an unfamiliar room furnished in the Chinese style. Martin was gazing down at me with a furrowed brow and Mrs Kendall was quietly taking my pulse.

"It's all right, Mrs Russell. You fainted, that's all. Caused by the heat in the attic, I expect. The constable kindly carried you in here. You were only out for a few minutes. Stay there quietly and rest for a little longer. The baby's fine."

Martin had actually carried me. I couldn't believe it: I was such a lump. Lifting me must have been difficult, I thought, chuckling to myself. At that moment the baby decided to turn over. I felt and watched my tummy bulge up at one side and then slither over to the other. 'Are you a boy or a girl?' I thought fleetingly, but it didn't matter at all, as long as the baby kept moving.

SOLICITING FROM HOME

After assuring himself that I was not likely to give birth there and then, Martin said his goodbyes and left.

"Since I'm here, Mrs Kendall, may I look at that stain on your bedroom ceiling?"

"I'm not sure you should take the stairs yet," she replied. "But I would be *most* appreciative if you would."

"I think I'll try," I said, pushing myself to my feet. That was fine, the room stayed still. I took a tentative step. No problem; the floor remained at the correct angle. I took another step, and another. "Yes, I'm alright. I'll take it slowly this time."

I was pleased I did, because it gave me time to survey the staircase. Mrs Kendall's half of the house contained the upper part of the original staircase, an elegant curved affair with a carved bannister and wide stairs with low rises. Beautiful paintings hung on the walls and a red Chinese cabinet graced the half-landing.

Her bedroom occupied the whole of the front of the first floor: another elegant room furnished in the colonial manner. Although the carpet was slightly worn, it was of thick Chinese silk and the colours were still fresh; it must have been stunning when it was new. The curtains, slightly faded where the sun had bleached them, were of leaf green Chinese silk and embroidered all over with flowers.

I noticed the strange smell at once — nauseatingly sweet with a rotten quality. I risked a glance upwards. Sure enough, a great dark stain covered half the ceiling. Amorphous and spreading, it might well have once represented the shape of a body — but then it could also have been Africa, clouds, or even, just possibly, a yacht. I wondered whether to take a deeper breath but quickly reflected that it was probably better not to push my luck, so after that one, brief glance and quick sniff, I made my way carefully back to the ground floor.

Mrs Kendall was waiting for me at the foot of the stairs. "Did you see the stain?" she asked. "Did you smell that dreadful stink?"

"I do see what you were complaining about, Mrs Kendall," I said, choosing my words with care. "It *does* appear that *something* has leaked through your ceiling from the roof space we've just seen next door. Do you have your deeds here, by any chance? If so, perhaps I could take them with me? Then I could check the legal situation with regard to the roof space, if you'd like?"

"No, Mrs Russell," she replied. "I keep the deeds at the bank, but I'll collect them from Mr Standish tomorrow. I do appreciate your kind offer."

"Thank you for taking care of me. I think I'll go home, now. If you have any more problems, do call Martin. I'm sure he'll come to help you. In the meantime, I'll see if there's anything I can do that will help."

"Thank you for coming," she responded, "And for taking me seriously. Not many people do."

- 6 -

I thought about many things as I walked slowly home, most of them connected to Mrs Kendall. My one overriding feeling was that I was missing something. Not surprising, I thought. I was still feeling sick and woozy although the fresh air was gradually restoring my senses.

'What made me faint?' I asked myself as I reflected on the suddenness of my collapse. 'I've never done *that* before.'

'Well, you did,' said the other, more reasonable, part of myself. 'Probably because you're pregnant and the weather's very hot. That loft was airless. And it was a very steep climb up those stairs.'

'Don't be stupid! I've never passed out in my life — even when I've had one too many — and I don't intend to start now.' This part of me wasn't feeling very reasonable. 'And there was a very peculiar smell up there, if you remember? Damp and fuggy — with something else behind it. Something I can't quite put my finger on.'

The memory of a sweetish, brackish odour permeating the loft combined with the recollection of the rotten smell in Mrs Kendall's bedroom seeped back into my nose, causing a renewed wave of nausea.

'Finger?' My reasonable self snorted. 'Nose, more like! Actually, there *was* an unusual smell. Something I haven't smelled for a long time.'

The more I tried to capture what had disturbed my olfactory organ, the more nauseated I felt and the more the odour seemed to drift away from my memory.

I turned into Fleece Street intending to take the slightly shorter way home.

"Good Morning, Mrs Russell — Melanie."

The call came from across the road. I could not mistake that greeting, nor the voice. I did my best to smile as Mr Standish, that kindest of bank managers, crossed over and shook my hand.

"I do hope you're well?" he enquired.

"Not very," I responded frankly, trying to breathe deeply as I fought the sudden heaving of my stomach. "I'm finding the heat a little difficult."

Mr Standish was all solicitude. "You've gone very white. Come over here, into the shade," he said, taking my arm and guiding me into the little public garden that edged this part of the street. "Sit down here for a while. Take the weight off your feet."

I sat down. I was very aware of the line of perspiration along my upper lip and the wetness under my fringe. He seated himself beside me and looked into my face with concern.

"Never known it so hot at this time of year," he remarked. "Early June and the temperature's already up in the eighties."

"I'm not used to carrying so much weight … nor having so little room to breathe." I tried to laugh, but it came out more like a sob.

"Oh, my dear," Mr Standish said, patting my hand. "Don't speak, just take a few deep breaths and you'll feel better in no time. If you don't mind an old man and four-times father giving you advice?" I had my eyes closed while I concentrated on using my breath to settle my stomach, so I simply nodded to indicate that I had no objection at all. "I suggest that you wear something cooler and preferably do not go out in the mid-day sun. You know: 'Mad Dogs and Englishmen' or, in your case, Englishwoman. *Not* a good idea."

"No, I know," I agreed, beginning to feel better. "I've been very silly. But I had to make an urgent site visit and it took longer than I expected."

I was not going to mention that I was blowed if I was going to buy any clothes that I would only wear for a month. I definitely had no intention of staying this size for long.

"I'm feeling much better, now," I smiled, and it was true. "It's not far home and I'm sure I'll make it."

"I'll escort you, just to make sure."

Mr Standish rose to his shinily-shod feet and offered me his arm. I heaved myself up and put my hand in the crook of his elbow. We set off slowly.

"Actually, I'm glad I've had the chance to speak to you away from the bank, Melanie. I was wondering how you were getting on? I know I've sent a few people along to you. Are you managing all right on your own? Do you need anything? A secretary, perhaps?"

"I'm doing fine at the moment, thank you, Mr Standish. I still haven't finally decided whether to set up my professional plate."

I used the old-fashioned words for setting up a legal practice. Solicitors were forbidden by their professional rules from advertising for business. It was permissible only to put up a small plate, usually brass, giving your name and profession; after that you simply waited for clients. As a solicitor, I was permitted to put one advertisement in a local newspaper indicating that an office was opening. That was all. The Solicitors' Practice Rules not only forbade me from advertising legal services but also forbade paying commission in return for introductions.

"I mention it because I saw a customer yesterday who has two small boys. She's a very experienced legal secretary, but she's been at home for the last six years." Mr Standish turned towards me. Magnified by his glasses, one eyelid fluttered. "She tells me she's looking for some part time work, now her youngest is starting school."

I laughed. "How kind of you to think of me, Mr Standish! I must admit I'm finding it a little difficult without a secretary. I'm not the world's fastest typist."

"Well then?"

"Not yet," I said hurriedly, "I haven't made a final decision. And I don't want to do more until I know how I'll cope with a baby."

"I think she'd be happy to do just a few hours if and when you need her."

"I really *do* appreciate the work that you've sent to me but I don't want to make any commitments to anyone."

"I understand," he said. "But when you change your mind ..."

We'd reached Rose Cottage, so I took my hand from his supporting arm. Wondering if it were permissible to kiss his cheek, I came to the swift conclusion that decorum

SOLICITING FROM HOME

demanded that I merely shake his hand.

"Thank you for looking after me, Mr Standish."

"Are you sure you're all right now?"

"I'm absolutely fine! But I won't be sorry to get back to my normal shape,"

Poppadum must have heard our voices because she started barking. Mr Standish watched me put my key in the lock and raised his voice to make himself heard above the din.

"Good. I'll leave you then. But before I go, I must tell you that Mr and Mrs White were very pleased that you completed their Wills so quickly. They said that they even understood what you were saying! In fact, they said they'd never before understood *what* a solicitor was talking about."

I could feel my grin spreading across my face. "Thank you so much for telling me."

Then I *did* kiss him. On the cheek — naturally.

The next day, Mrs Kendall collected the deeds to her property from the bank and brought them to me in a fat buff deed packet wound around with red cotton tape that tied in a bow at the front.

I was delighted to find that her legal title to the property was not registered at the Land Registry and that it consisted of a bundle of handwritten deeds, many of which were written on parchment. I loved looking at old unregistered deeds and piecing together the legal title. It was so much more interesting — and fascinating — than a registered title to land. Perhaps I should explain that the phrase *legal title* is more easily understood as *entitlement in law*.

Under ancient English law, title to land was required to

be evidenced in writing. Its ownership changed when the land was bought and sold, or 'conveyed', from the seller to the purchaser. Thus, the written document that evidenced the change became known as a 'Deed of Conveyance' (or simply a 'Conveyance'); and the process of transferring the legal title from one person to another became known as 'conveyancing'. Of course, there were other ways that ownership changed, one of the most common being by way of a gift in the Will of someone who had died, in which case the appropriate deed was called an Assent.

However, the Land Registration Act was enacted in 1925 with the intention of giving state-guaranteed legal title to everyone who owned a registrable interest in land. Under the terms of this Act, state registration of title became compulsory on the sale and purchase of land, but, because there were so many titles to be registered in England and Wales, registration was brought in gradually, district by district. The county of Kent was designated early on as an area of compulsory registration of title. Thus on Romney Marsh registration had become compulsory in 1958, while nearby in rural Sussex registration did not become compulsory until the early 1970s.

In practice, registration of Oldchurch property was compulsory. But this was only if it were *sold* after 1958. If the property's ownership passed for some other reason, then registration was not required.

I soon discovered that Old Owlers had been in Mrs. Kendall's family for generations. In fact, my client owned part of one of the oldest houses in Oldchurch. She had inherited it shortly after the War when it had passed to her under the terms of her uncle's Will, and it therefore followed that the legal title to the property was not registered.

Because the title was unregistered, it was necessary to 'prove' the title by tracing the consecutive ownership of the land through the written documents or deeds contained in the bundle Mrs Kendall had given me. Recently, the period of ownership for which the law required evidence of ownership had been reduced to fifteen years but, in my opinion, it was still preferable to follow the old requirement of a thirty year title.

What I loved about this part of the work of conveyancing was that it was a combination of detective work and re-assembling history. The old deeds, handwritten on vellum in ink, were beautiful, although difficult to decipher. Land was often described as a 'piece or parcel' comprising a certain acreage or describing the boundaries by reference to the ownership of adjoining land. Where there was a plan, it was invariably hand-drawn and usually not to scale. Over time, the old estates were broken down into smaller parts. In the nineteenth century, there had been a profusion of building developments. These often necessitated the provision of complicated arrangements and covenants with which both the purchaser and vendor, and their subsequent successors in title, had to comply.

I settled down to enjoy the mystery of Old Owlers. Reading through the documents, juggling from one plan to another, I pieced together the legal history of the house and drew a map of connections. Some of the documents went back hundreds of years, hand written on large sheets of parchment. My fingers smoothed the ancient vellum, stiff yet fragile with age. Folded, the documents were about the size of the deed packet and a little squarer than foolscap, but when eased open they were immense. Much of the writing was difficult to decipher. Extra tails and double S's looped across the whole surface making it more challenging to read than the more common round-hand or copperplate. Reluctantly, I re-folded the old documents and put them to one side: they were ancient history and I needed to look at the more recent past.

Although the title was complicated, I managed to piece the patchwork of deeds together, comparing plans as the land boundaries shifted and changed over the centuries. Old Owlers had passed through various hands. Some of the lands it originally possessed were sold to a neighbouring farm and some of those were re-acquired later. Adjoining parcels of land were purchased and added to the title. There were Abstracts of Title, Indentures, Conveyances, Deeds of Mortgage, Deeds of Second Mortgage, Receipts, Releases, Official Copies of Probate, Assents, Deeds of Rentcharge, a Deed of Arrangement, Assessments of Tithes, Leases, Counterpart Leases, Surrenders of Lease and assorted other deeds and documents.

The last Conveyance was dated 1923 and conveyed the whole house and garden, with the farmland it then possessed, to Arthur Chapman, Mrs Kendall's uncle. As I refolded the deed, I noticed a tightly-written memorandum dated 1932 recording the grant of a long lease of ninety-nine years. It was a very ordinary memorandum but I read it carefully. It was clear that the lease related to part of the house known as Old Owlers. But there was a problem. The memorandum was missing a plan, so it was unclear as to exactly which part had been leased.

Frowning, I searched through the remaining deeds.

SOLICITING FROM HOME

Eventually, I came across the missing plan folded inside another document. I could hardly believe my eyes. I checked three times before I telephoned Mrs Kendall.

After we had exchanged the usual pleasantries, I said: "I'm pleased to say that I've perused the deeds to Old Owlers — and I've found something very interesting. Unfortunately, the situation is rather too complicated to explain over the telephone. I wonder whether we could meet? This afternoon, perhaps?"

She agreed and we arranged a time. Afterwards, I sat down to go through the Deeds for a fourth time and made some extra notes so that, by the time we met, I would have something to refer to.

- 7 -

What I had discovered was a curious fact: Mrs Kendall was living in the wrong part of the house. The Deans were living in the part that technically belonged to Mrs Kendall. It was difficult to explain this simple truth in layman's terms. But I did my best.

"If I hadn't been through this so carefully I'd suspect it was the product of an over-active imagination," I told her. "But please bear with me."

Mrs Kendall smiled tightly. "Actually that sounds very intriguing," she said. "Please go on."

"I know that you said you had inherited the house from your uncle. That's absolutely right of course. His name was Arthur Chapman and I have a copy of the Probate of his Will and an Assent which make it clear that your title to the property known as Old Owlers is perfectly in order, but ..."

"I knew there had to be a 'but'!" she declared and then went on hastily: "Don't let me stop you."

"I presume from the date of your uncle's death, in 1944, that you did not even *see* your part of the house until after the War when you came back from Singapore?"

"Well, we used to visit my uncle there when I was a child, but that was before it was divided."

"Quite. And I presume you were on your best behaviour and didn't run around the place, investigating the attics and cellars?"

"Oh no! Quite the opposite! My cousins, my brother and

SOLICITING FROM HOME

I used to read in the attics and play all sorts of games in the cellars." Her face softened in a nostalgic far-away smile. "I was a tomboy, you know, when I had the chance. My mother used to call me The Hoyden! You probably don't know this, but old smugglers passages used to run from the cellars to the church and the adjoining houses. We had wonderful adventures and games of make-believe. We always hoped to find some treasure but we never did. The old passages are all filled in now, of course."

"What a pity you can only enter the attics from the Deans' half of the house. I think it's the same with the cellars isn't it?"

"Yes, I remember there was a trapdoor in the pantry floor. But I gather that all the cellars were filled in after the War — the back of the property was damaged, you see, and the rubble was deposited into the cellars to make a firm base on which to re-build the back wall. What a pity! I had such an attachment to those cellars."

"This is rather strange, I admit, but I'm sure what I'm about to tell you is correct. When your uncle inherited the property in the nineteen twenties, Old Owlers was one dwelling but, probably because of the economic depression, it was divided into two residences in the nineteen thirties — one of which was sold." I paused.

"Yes, I know *that*," she interrupted, almost scornfully

"Of course. But this is where it gets complicated. Shall we call your part of the house 'A' and the Deans' part 'B'?"

"If you must," she said, clearly humouring me

"Your uncle kept part A and sold B."

She nodded.

"Now, the interesting thing is that there's what's called 'a Reservation' in the Conveyance — that's the Conveyance of B to a Mr John Dean — reserving the right for the owners of A to use the cellar below and the roof space above B."

"So?"

"The Deans, or whoever owned B at the time, must have swapped one half of the property for the other. You are actually living in the half that was conveyed away. *You* are living in B — and Nancy's living in A."

"But how could that possibly be?" Mrs Kendall was looking amazed.

"Have you ever seen the deeds before now?" Mrs Kendall shook her head in a dazed fashion. "No, I didn't think so. I expect your uncle's solicitor sent them straight to the bank for safekeeping?" She nodded. "I see his firm was based up in Leeds. He would have made sure your title to the property was correct and in order. That's all he had to do. The title *is* in order. He would have had no reason to think that the wrong half was empty, would he?"

"No, I suppose not."

"And so you simply moved into the part that was vacant."

"That's right," she said after a few seconds' consideration. "David Dean's parents were living in the other side. I don't think I even thought about which side was mine. There was no need to. Are you sure about this?"

"There's a Memorandum endorsed on the back of the Conveyance to your uncle. It's in very small insignificant handwriting and easily overlooked. Originally there was a plan attached as well, but it had come away. I found it wedged inside the lease of A. That was the other part of the puzzle."

"A lease? I thought I owned the freehold."

"Yes, you do, have no fear. Your uncle did, too, but he didn't live there all his life. In 1936 he leased his part A — which is the property you own — for seven years to a Mr John Dean."

Mrs Kendall shook her head. "I'm still a little confused. Are you saying that the Deans have a lease of the property I'm living in?"

"No, I'm saying they *had* a lease which has expired. And that lease was of the part they are currently occupying but which you actually own. They just stayed in the part which had the entrance to the roof space and the cellar and allowed you to move in to the smaller part."

"Let me get this clear. You're saying I'm living in the wrong part of the property?"

"Precisely."

"So I own the bigger part and the attic?"

"Yes. The attic is yours. And, if it still exists, the cellar does too."

"And you say the Deans own the part I'm living in?"

"Yes, and no — just to confuse you! You still own the freehold of their part but subject to a lease for ninety-nine years from 1932. In other words their lease has another fifty-five years to run. Then the whole property will be yours."

She snorted. "I'm not likely to live that long!"

"No, maybe not, but you *will* be able to leave your interest under your Will."

"I'll take your word for that. But the most important

question is — what do we do now?"

It was a very good question and one which I had anticipated.

"As I've said, I'm certain that you and the Deans are living in each other's properties. If you had decided to sell your part, the truth of the matter would have come to light as soon as your solicitor looked at your title deeds prior to drafting the contract for sale. The same would have applied had the Deans decided to sell their half. You both have a legally enforceable right against the other."

"So what would have been the outcome if I had wanted to sell Old Owlers?"

"I suppose it would have been necessary to take the matter to Court. Actually, you could do that now, were you minded to."

"I thought so."

"But, in my opinion, to go to Court about this would be taking a sledgehammer to crack a nut. It would be expensive, time-consuming and very uncomfortable on a personal level, since it seems that there is no love lost between you and the Deans."

"You're right about that!"

"My suggestion is that we save a great deal of time, money and trouble by working out a compromise which would suit you *and* be acceptable to the Deans. If that doesn't work, we always have recourse to litigation."

She pondered for a minute or two while I smiled encouragingly and then, because she was still scowling at the ceiling in thought, I resorted to scribbling a few more notes on my pad.

"Would you do that?" she asked eventually.

SOLICITING FROM HOME

"Of course!" I said, trying to hide my excitement. I was sure something similar must have happened somewhere else at sometime previously, but I was aware that such a mistake — if it was a mistake — was most uncommon. I knew, too, that I would derive a great deal of satisfaction from resolving the situation, especially if I could find a way of doing it without ruffling too many feathers.

One of the things I most enjoyed about being a country solicitor was the chance to make a real difference to the lives of ordinary people by unravelling their interesting and knotty problems. Admittedly, Mrs Kendall's explosion into my home had shown that she was not an ordinary person, but, on reflection, ordinary seemed a most disparaging term. Each client who consulted me was different and so were the matters they brought to me for legal advice.

After some discussion, Mrs Kendall and I figured out an arrangement that would suit her, was fair to the Deans, and would also give them sufficient time to take legal advice if they decided to do so.

No sooner had I made a note of these points in my notebook than Mrs Kendall leapt to her feet, declaring: "There's no time like the present! Let's go now. I'm sure either Nancy or David — or perhaps both of them since it's a Friday — will be there."

I was reluctant to move so fast, but there seemed nothing to be gained from delay. I wrote a quick note for Ryan, put Poppadum on her lead, and accompanied Mrs Kendall back to Old Owlers.

As we approached the door, we heard voices raised in argument. Mrs Kendall and I exchanged glances.

"They're always at it hammer and tongs," she said. "I

don't think it means any …."

She was interrupted by a thump, a scream and a loud bang. The next moment the front door flew open and Nancy flew out clutching her head, closely followed by a short stocky man with dark hair and an even darker scowl. He raised his fists when he saw us standing there, staring.

"What're *you* looking at?" he sneered. "Ain't you ever seen a proper bloke before?"

As he came closer I smelled the beer on his breath — and the body odour from the hairy armpits revealed by his sleeveless vest. Repulsed and annoyed, I drew myself up to my full five feet eight inches and looked down my upward-turned nose.

"Personally, I don't consider you anything but a bully," I said. "I suggest you go inside and sleep off whatever you've been drinking. Don't worry about your wife. We'll look after her."

I threw a glance towards Mrs Kendall, who'd put her arm round Nancy.

A sudden gust of stale sweat and beer made me duck instinctively. A fist brushed past my head as I twisted to the left. My would-be attacker had obviously expected his fist to connect and the impetus of his intended blow threw him off balance. Uttering a stream of profanities, he veered forward, lost his footing, and crashed down on his face into the gutter.

I felt like kicking him — and I'd already drawn my foot back before I realised that to kick him when he was flat on his face would reduce me to his level. Disdain was a preferable reaction. I stepped over his prone body and hastened after the two women into Mrs Kendall's hall.

SOLICITING FROM HOME

In a way, I was glad Dave had taken a swipe at me because it gave me ammunition against him. I recalled the heavy make-up that Nancy had been wearing the previous day; make up that I felt sure was an attempt to hide the evidence of a beating.

I was aware that many wives who were assaulted by their husbands were either too fearful or too submissive to make a complaint to the authorities. Others were too scared for their children. I knew, too, that the police were inclined to look the other way in matters of domestic violence, considering it a personal matter and not a crime. However, threatening me with violence in the open street, in front of witnesses, was quite another matter.

If I could not persuade Nancy to report her husband to the police, I would have no compunction in doing so myself. In fact, I decided I would complain to the police whatever Nancy did. Whether actual or threatened, violence towards a woman, especially in the last trimester of pregnancy, was beyond the pale of civilised behaviour. It was only my innate sense of self-preservation that had saved me from being floored by her husband.

While these thoughts were racing through my mind, Mrs Kendall had once more come into her own. She locked the front door behind us; checked Nancy's bleeding face; made sure she was safely seated with her feet up on the sofa; commanded me to keep watch over her; and dashed into the kitchen for ice.

I commandeered the telephone and rang Martin at the police station. By the time I had apprised him of what had occurred, Dave Dean was shouting through the keyhole and thumping on the door. The noise caused Nancy to shrivel into herself, brought Mrs Kendal out of the kitchen with a bag of frozen peas for Nancy's bruised forehead, and made Martin decide to call for reinforcements.

"I'm on my way," he said.

"Good!" I put the receiver back on its rest.

"You fucking interfering women," Dave yelled, the slurred words full of threat. "You can't get away with this! Give me my bloody wife back. Nancy, you get out here! NOW!"

I'm not sure why I did what I did, then — it was stupid and foolhardy, but anger overcame reason. He was leaning against the door, shouting more obscenities. I unlocked it and jerked it hard inwards. He fell sprawling at my feet in a welter of limbs and curses. Holding his head, which had hit the door jamb, he dragged himself to his feet and swayed towards me, swearing. But I'd had more than enough of Mr David Dean and my rage exploded so violently and so suddenly that he reeled back before me.

"How dare you!" I shouted, my face an inch from his despite his reeking breath. "How dare you! You horrible little man. Shut your face and go back in the hole where you belong!"

A look of horror crossed his face, quickly followed by a leer.

"Shut up yourself, you slut," he shouted. "Some bloke obviously fucked you, and fucked you well. You need putting in your place and I'm the man to do it."

The leer became a sneer. He lurched towards me and made a grab for my hair. I felt the red mist rise before my eyes. People who knew me as a child never pulled my hair, the one thing that always made me see red. Mr Dean had

SOLICITING FROM HOME

made a serious mistake. Before I knew it, I felt my hands ball into fists and my eyes blaze. I took a step forward. He took a step back.

"Man? Man, you say?" I took another step forward: he retreated a step. "You're not a man! You're a disgrace." It was a strange sort of dance this, as I advanced and he retreated to the rhythm of my rage. "Yes, that's what you are — a disgrace to your sex! How your wife has put up with you, I have no idea. You aren't good enough to lick her shoe."

He puffed himself up, opened his mouth as if to respond, but instead blanched, heaved and threw up the contents of his stomach. Luckily he had retreated far enough so that his vomit only spattered my shoes, but I was in full flow, and disgust and revulsion overcame me.

"You are revolting! Disgusting!" I pushed him. "Get away from me." I pushed him harder. "Get away from here." And he slipped in his vomit, almost fell, saved himself, slipped again, and landed face down on the path. At least he was outside the house. He looked so small and pathetic that my rage deflated as fast as it had grown. I threw him a look of loathing mixed with spite and had my final say.

"You poor little boy. Go home and clean yourself up. And when you've done that you can clear up your mess here, too!"

I closed the door. Suddenly I found myself trembling and feeling faint — no doubt the effect of the adrenalin rush caused by my sudden rage.

Normally, I was very seldom angry. On the contrary, I was known as the peacemaker who always tried to pour oil on troubled water. Not much oil about this, I thought, more like petrol — and the thought made me giggle stupidly although I could not stay still. I walked backward and forward, the baby kicking me hard. My breath was coming in huge gasps. as I waited for the final flames of my anger to subside.

When I turned my gaze on the other women in the room it was to see them watching me in silent amazement. At least, I thought it was amazement, but it was probably horror. Next moment, someone knocked on the door — and there was Martin, wearing his helmet and holding a well-coated David Dean by one arm. The arm was pushed up his back, and David was bent nearly double. Martin was trying to keep his body and nose from any further contact with his prisoner, as well as to side-step the pool of vomit on the doorstep. None of this was easy, but Martin had an air of resignation: I supposed it was all in a day's work for him.

"This is the man you complained about, I believe, Mrs Russell? I need to make sure before I take him to the cells to sober up."

"That is the person, Constable," I said.

"Indeed he is, Constable," Mrs. Kendall butted in, striking a commanding figure. "He has been terrorising us all, shouting through the letterbox and banging on the door. And, when he is sober, I would appreciate your instructing him not to come near me. If he does, I shall instruct Mrs. Russell to apply to the Court for an injunction to restrain him from doing so."

"He's been beating me up for years, Martin," a small trembling voice offered from the direction of the sofa. We all turned to see Nancy's wan face, washed clear by tears and

SOLICITING FROM HOME

ice of its disguising make up, so that old bruises and new black eye were all clearly visible. "Can you hold him for a few days so that I can take the children away to my sister's?"

"It's a domestic, Nancy, not a crime. So it's a civil matter, not something the police deal with, I'm afraid."

"Surely, you can do something?" she begged.

"I'm afraid not. Ask Mrs Russell."

"Actually, Constable, Mr Dean has committed an assault. Not only on his wife. Against me, too. And I fully intend to lay charges against him."

Martin sighed. "Very well, Mrs Russell, I'll hold him overnight. If you wish to press charges, please come along to the Police Station as soon as possible to give a statement. Are you going to come quietly, Dave? Or do I have to demonstrate my superior strength?"

Dave shrugged what was visible of his shoulders. Martin released the arm-lock, whilst keeping a firm hold of the arm. With practised ease, David Dean was handcuffed and led away, chastened but still muttering oaths and threats.

- 8 -

Nancy breathed a huge sigh of relief and her shoulders sagged. Now that her husband had gone, all strength seemed to have deserted her. From her previously complaisant manner, I suspected that she had been brutalised by the bully for some considerable time. Her eyes were squeezed shut and despair hung about her in a heavy cloud, but she was clinging for dear life to Mrs Kendall's comforting hand. The latter sat beside her on the sofa and gently stroked Nancy's brow with her free hand.

"There, there, my dear," she soothed. "You need some rest. Come upstairs and lie down for half an hour. I'll ring the doctor and get him to come and give you a once-over."

Nancy's eyes shot open. "Lie down? Oh, I'd love to but I can't! What's the time? I have to pick the children up."

"It's half-past three. What time does school end?"

A succession of emotions flitted across Nancy's face — worry, exhaustion, fear, and finally relief.

"Thank Goodness! I arranged for a friend to give them their tea today, but I can't leave them there too long. I wanted them out of the way so I could have it out with Dave." She paused, swallowed and tears streamed down her cheeks. "I'm so sorry, Catherine. So sorry. We've been so horrid to you. And you've been so kind to me today."

She choked on the words. But she needed to speak and, once she began, words flooded from her mouth.

"It's been so hard. *So* hard. I can't tell you. I've been so worried, so frightened. For myself, of course, but even more

SOLICITING FROM HOME

for the children. They're very scared of Dave — he's become so unapproachable and erratic. Isn't it awful when your children are frightened of their father and there's nothing you can do to change things? He wasn't always like this. He was lovely, full of fun and always laughing. And we were so happy."

She allowed herself a fleeting smile at the memory and then her mouth twisted into a grimace.

"That was before *they* got hold of him and turned him into a junkie. It started slowly, of course. Just a little weed at the weekend, and then, more recently, something stronger. Then I came home one day and heard him hammering up in the attic. He said he had a project, that he was converting the loft into a playroom. He didn't tell me what sort of playroom! I walked in from work one day and found him lugging fluorescent bulbs up the stairs. Far too many, I thought. I said so. But he laughed and said I must leave it to him. He said I'd be pleased if I knew how much money he would be making. Even then I didn't twig."

She took a long shuddering breath. "You see he'd been smoking more and more weed each week. His temper was so unpredictable, I found it best to keep a low profile. I was becoming scared to talk to him, he was off his head so often. He spent more and more time in the loft. And when he wasn't in the loft he'd be round the pub. He drank more and more. He came staggering home each night. When I tried to remonstrate with him — or to tell him that the children needed their father — he'd use his fists on me. Eventually, I stopped saying anything to him. I'd cook but he wouldn't eat. He was wasted most of the time. He was always late for work. In fact, he stopped going to work at all, but he didn't tell me. There seemed to be enough money — but where did it come from?"

Speaking had calmed her. She looked from one to the other of us beseechingly. "You know don't you? I knew, of course, I just couldn't admit it. One evening when he was down the pub I crept upstairs with the bolt cutters. He'd padlocked the door to the loft, you see. And you know what I found? Plants. Cannabis. Growing all through the roof. And there was this poor terrified boy there too. When he saw me his eyes popped out of his head and he peed himself all over the floor. I swear I never knew he was there — but I saw a sort of bed. He must have been living up there. And I never knew! I swear I never knew!"

Her eyes grew wide and wild and she shook. With fear? Remorse? I couldn't tell, but I did believe that she had blinded herself to what was going on until she made the discovery.

"When Dave came home that night, I was waiting for him. I had cried myself silly and then I'd made a decision. It was the weed or me. And if I left, I'd take the children with me. I couldn't live like that any longer and I didn't want my children living in fear, never knowing what temper their father would be in. Luckily for me, when he came home, Dave was a bit the worse for drink — enough to make him amorous — but he wasn't high. When I told him my decision, he cried, promised to make it right. I said everything must go — and go the very next day. He told me he had lost his job. He'd been sacked because he was so unreliable. I cried. He cried."

Tears sprang to her eyes and she sniffed hard. "And the next day he began the dismantling. I don't know what happened to the boy. His bedding and he had both gone when I went up there that evening. The plants had gone, too. We worked together, clearing the apparatus from the loft. And then we cleaned the whole area thoroughly. That was only a couple of weeks before you came and asked to inspect the attic. Perfect timing. There was nothing there, as you saw, and you brought Martin, who also saw that it was empty."

I couldn't resist a cry of triumph. "So I was right when I had a feeling the loft had been recently vacated. And that was the smell that made me faint! Cannabis!"

"The blokes he was working for found somewhere else to grow the stuff. They'd heard on the grapevine that you, Catherine…" She looked at Mrs Kendall. "…suspected something was going on. Time to move, they said. But they had Dave hooked on heroin by this time and he needed his fix. They turned the screw — and got him involved in something else, something far worse."

"And because he felt guilty, he started arguments with you so that he could beat you up and keep you quiet?" I suggested.

"Something like that, perhaps."

"What is he involved in now?"

"I don't know. I *really* don't know. He is frightened and moody, violent at the least provocation. That puts us all on edge. The children and I have been walking on eggshells again for the past week. Today, Dave cut himself shaving and Dan asked — quite innocently — why Dave had blood on his face. Dave smacked him round the head again and again. I thought he was going to kill him. I pushed in front of Dan and Dave hit me — intentionally. You could see that by the rage in his eyes. Sally was screaming. I grabbed them both and took them along to my friend Janet who agreed to keep them until I called for them. I was angry and fed up. I couldn't live in fear a moment longer. I confronted him — and you saw what happened."

"Yes, we did," Mrs Kendall and I said in unison.

A strange quietness fell as we each followed our own thoughts. Nancy's sniffs and muffled sobs broke into the quietness. Mrs Kendall was lost in thought and my brain was working overtime as I considered how Nancy's revelations would impact on the situation with the two parts of Old Owlers.

Mrs Kendall recovered first.

"Well," she said briskly. "It's good to know that I'm not completely mad. Or even as mad as others seemed to believe! But we can deal with that later. The most important thing to do now is to decide how we can help Nancy and the children. What do you think, Mrs Russell?"

"I agree," I said, bowled over by her magnanimous attitude. "At least Martin has Dave in custody. It's likely that tomorrow he will either be released on bail or remanded in custody by the Magistrates Court. Tonight you can relax a little, Nancy, and decide what you will do."

She made no reply. Her sobs doubled in intensity, but I wasn't prepared to let the matter drop.

"I'm sure you know that what you've told us is very serious. You could end up in gaol yourself for aiding and abetting Dave in possessing and supplying drugs, and then what would happen to your children? You need to think of them."

"I know. I can't think straight. Tell me what to do," she

SOLICITING FROM HOME

implored. The sobs were subsiding but tears continued to stream down her cheeks.

"There's only one thing you can do. Tell the police all you know. Make a clean breast of it — and be prepared to give evidence against Dave."

She took a deep shuddering breath, shut her eyes and shook her head.

"There's no other way," Mrs Kendall waded in. "You *must* listen to Mrs Russell. For the children's sake if not your own."

"If I could find another way, I'd tell you," I assured Nancy. "But you know you have to do it. I'll come with you, if you like."

"That's kind of you." Nancy sighed with deep weariness. "I'll take you up on that offer. She glanced at the clock. Shall we go now?"

For the second time that day I agreed that there was no time like the present. I checked my watch, too. I wanted to be home in time to make supper because Ryan liked to have a meal on the table when he came in from work, and I was fast running out of time to prepare something edible—even if that something was only the inevitable salad that marked this, the hottest summer on record.

"Yes," I agreed tersely. "Let's get it over and done with, so you can collect the children before it gets too late."

Mrs Kendall passed a box of tissues to Nancy. "The bathroom's upstairs. You will want to wash your face before you go."

When Nancy left the room, Mrs Kendall turned to me.

"We can leave the question of ownership of the property for now," she said. "Nancy has enough to think about for the present."

"How kind of you to see it that way," I said, realising that my feelings towards Mrs Kendall had changed completely. When she'd first knocked on my door, I'd feared that she was insane: now I knew beyond doubt that her eccentric manner hid a warm heart and a very knowledgeable efficiency, as well as a real understanding of human nature. I felt that I was the one who was wet behind the ears — everything I thought I knew I had learned from law books. Mrs Kendall had run a hospital in a foreign country, had been captured by the Japanese and almost died in the prisoner of war camp. I came to learn later that she had taken charge of her fellow prisoners, more of whom had survived under her leadership than in any other camp. She had been moulded by the arena of war. No wonder she expected respect. From that moment on, she had mine. In fact, we became good friends.

This was the beginning of my involvement in these events, but whereas the beginning unfolded over the course of a few days, the matters themselves were not completely resolved for some years.

Nancy and I went together to the Police Station where we laid separate charges against Dave Dean for assault and battery. Nancy also made a Statement about the circumstances she had revealed to me and Mrs Kendall. Within hours, police were crawling all over Nancy's home and they soon found sufficient evidence to confirm her Statement.

In due course, a drug ring was uncovered that extended all the way along the south coast. In the course of the police search, a large package wrapped in black plastic was

SOLICITING FROM HOME

discovered beneath the floorboards in the attic. At first, Nancy feared it might prove to be the body of the boy she had seen there, but it turned out to be a stash of compost. After it was removed the smell in Mrs Kendall's bedroom diminished and the mark on the ceiling gradually faded, to be eventually covered with a layer of fresh paint, and forgotten.

As I had surmised, Nancy was called to give evidence against Dave and his co-defendants. By then, some eighteen months later, she was well on the way to recovery, thanks to Mrs Kendall.

The elderly woman took Nancy and her children under her wing, accommodating them in her own home. In time, she became an honorary grandmother to them all, and when she died five years later she willed her whole Estate to Nancy.

These events kept me busy for some time. A few days after my baby, Sarah-Jane, was born, I found myself in Court as a witness as well as needing to give Nancy support through the preliminary hearings relating to the charges against Dave. When the case was eventually brought to Court for trial, the hearing was at the Old Bailey, as it had been found that the gang had tendrils that reached throughout England. Twenty people were arraigned with Dave and they were all given long prison sentences. I accompanied Nancy, who was once again required to give evidence and was very nervous. She acquitted herself well but later, in private, sobbed on my shoulder for the person Dave had been, the one she loved, the father of her children — but she knew that she had to break free of him.

She instructed me to handle her divorce proceedings

against him and I managed to persuade the Court to order that Dave's share in Old Owlers be transferred to her. I handled the transfer, too.

Eventually, when Mrs Kendall considered it appropriate, I explained to Nancy that she and Mrs Kendall were in occupation of each other's part of the house. But by then the two women were so attached to each other that they decided not to move. Instead they simply removed the partition that had divided Old Owlers in two and used the house as a single dwelling.

I was invited to their joint housewarming party and it was good to experience the feeling of happy contentment which pervaded the old house. With the resilience of children, Dan and Sally soon settled back at school, and became happy beneficiaries of the fondness between the two former enemies. I found it hard to pass by Old Owlers without smiling at the fortunate outcome of a dreadful time.

There was an interesting postscript to these events. Six months before Mrs Kendall died, police made a dawn raid on two adjoining semi-detached houses close to Old Owlers. They discovered that the houses were at the centre of a people-trafficking operation, being 'safe' houses where illegal immigrants — mostly Pakistanis as Mrs Kendall had asserted so long previously — could lie hidden in the joint roof space for a few days. Later, at dead of night, they would be transferred into lorries and despatched to London.

Once again, a noted gang of criminals was involved; and once again Mrs Kendall's lips bore a smile of satisfaction, it having been proved beyond doubt that she had been right to fear for the victims of what she called a 'terrible trade'.

- 9 -

A day or so after my run-in with Dave Dean it was time for my routine pregnancy check-up. Myles gave me the once-over, confirmed that all was well with both me and the baby and, telling me that he had something he wanted to ask me, invited me to join him for lunch at the local pub. The Woolsack had the advantage of being right next door to the surgery. It also boasted a walled garden and good beer. Myles escorted me to the former and went in search of a pint for himself. I settled for homemade ginger beer — a non-alcoholic alternative to my usual half pint of bitter.

I made straight for my favourite corner of the garden where a table had been placed under the spreading branches of a copper beech tree close to the warm-red brick wall of the boundary. That particular place was also the coolest; the day was as hot as its predecessor and I had no intention of fainting again. Sinking onto a cushioned wooden chair, I put my feet up on another, closing my eyes and letting the peace of the place wash over me.

Here in the centre of the little town of Oldchurch all I could hear was the buzzing of the bees and the song of a blackbird hidden in the tree above me. The scent of wallflowers floated on the breeze which rustled the dark red leaves of the tree. I sighed with contentment, rejoicing in my luck to be here on a 'working' day and relieved of any undue cares about my pregnancy.

The Woolsack was a medieval building and its front elevation to the High Street had hardly changed in four hundred years, but at the rear it had been extended and extended again over the centuries, so that the roof was not one but many, of different sizes and at differing heights from the ground, their one common factor being red Kentish peg tiles spotted with moss. The walls were painted white and interlaced with such a webbing of black beams, drainpipes and gutters that the overall impression was of a cat's cradle.

Window boxes and a plethora of hanging baskets, suspended from every available surface by wrought iron brackets, were full to overflowing with sweetly scented pansies and heartsease, their brightly-painted yellow and violet faces set off by a backdrop of dark green variegated ivy. In a semi-circular flower bed beneath, the last of the season's tulips blazed in red and gold. In this haven of fragrance, the scent of wallflowers was most pervasive. Looking around, I saw they were growing along the top of the old wall. Others were clinging to the nooks and crannies along the edge of the wall, where the mower could not reach.

A door closed with a sharp click and Myles came out, bearing a frothing tankard in one hand, a glass of fizzing liquid in the other and a menu tucked under his arm. I hurriedly lowered my feet. Myles made his way along the uneven narrow brick path behind the tulips and across the sea of unevenly mown grass. As he placed the drinks on the table, I pulled the menu from under his arm.

"Thank you," I said, with feeling. "I'm parched — actually, I'm famished, too. Cheers!"

I raised my ginger beer in salute and gulped down a third of it. It was cool and delicious.

"Me, too. Cheers!" He grinned, raising his tankard. He

SOLICITING FROM HOME

downed half his pint and deftly wiped the froth from his top lip with the back of his hand. "That was good. Now what will you have to eat?"

I had been studying the menu eagerly so my decision was instantaneous.

"Chilli-con-carne please."

"*Chilli-con-carne?* Are you sure?"

"Absolutely. I need something spicy."

"Spicy eh? You must be carrying a boy. Well, we have to humour you at the moment, I suppose. Though I think you might find it a bit indigestible?"

"No, it'll be fine. Honestly," I insisted.

"Right, I'll go and order. I'll be back in a jiffy."

I leaned back, closing my eyes again. I drifted into a daydream on the perfume of wallflowers.

"A very odd thing happened to me yesterday."

The words were spoken close to me. A man's voice, light in timbre.

Startled, I jerked awake and looked around. A young couple had taken one of the tables near the tulips but they were leaning across their table, holding hands and speaking in tones inaudible to me. Otherwise the garden was empty. The voice must have come from behind the wall: no doubt its owner was unaware that he could be overheard.

"Really? What was it?" Another man's voice, this one deep and melodious. It sounded familiar but I couldn't quite place it.

The first voice came again, hesitantly now. He sounded older than the other. "I'm a little embarrassed to tell you. It was *so* strange. I'm sure you'll think I imagined it."

"No, I can assure you I won't. You should know me well enough to know that, Stephen."

The owner of the second voice was clearly as intrigued as I, and then I remembered who it was — my friend, the local dentist, Tom Williams. "Please, do go on," Tom urged. "I promise I'll keep it under my hat."

"I'm not sure where to start. Let me see …" Stephen sounded uneasy. "Do you recall me telling you that the house Deeds spoke of an old well in the garden?"

"Yes, of course I do. You thought it must be hidden under something. A rockery, I think?"

"Yes. An odd place for such a large rockery, I always thought. Do you remember? That brick path led to it and then stopped short."

"I remember," Tom assured him. "But it looks different now."

Stephen snorted. "Indeed it does! While you were away on holiday I thought I'd investigate. I got out my dowsing rods to dowse for the well and, sure enough, they indicated water at a depth of some thirty feet." Stephen's voice trailed off.

"Where?" Tom prodded.

"Beneath the rockery."

"Aha! So what did you do?"

Stephen made an odd sound between a grunt and a chuckle. "I waited till Mary was out for the day and then I dismantled the rockery. It took a brave man to do that without asking her, I can tell you! However, I took my courage in both hands and removed the plants. To my surprise, I found that they were planted in amongst a load of

SOLICITING FROM HOME

bricks, as if a building had previously stood there and collapsed."

"Interesting. Do you think it once housed the well?"

"I didn't know, so I got the rods out and dowsed again. And again the rods indicated that there was water below. So I laboured away, piling all the bricks up in one place and tiles in another, and removing the rest of the rubbish and earth. I'd only just finished when Mary came home. She was livid! Wouldn't speak to me for hours because I'd demolished her precious rockery."

"That doesn't surprise me."

"No, I probably deserved it. But what I haven't told you, is that when I'd moved everything away, I discovered an iron coffin-like arrangement bolted down, rusted somewhat and impossible to budge. I didn't let Mary see that. I covered it over with dirt and waited … and waited … and waited until she was out for the day at her sister's." Stephen paused again. "That was yesterday."

He stopped speaking. Tom (and I) waited. The silence grew unbearably until Tom asked: "So what happened yesterday?"

"I rushed down the garden as soon as she'd gone. I cleared the earth away, and then I had to wrestle with the iron lid. After a struggle, I managed to break the hinges and lever up the top. Sure enough, underneath there was a bricked shaft, covered by a round metal lid." He swallowed uncomfortably. "The lid was difficult to budge, too. In the end I took a hammer to the lid and levered it up. I was really sweating by this time, as you can imagine! So I went in for a glass of water. While I was indoors I checked the time to see how long it would be before Mary came back. It was ten past three."

"What time does she normally get back?" Tom asked.

"About six."

"So you had plenty of time for exploration?"

"Yes, that's what I thought. I went straight back outside and stood looking down the well. The sun was blazing and it seemed very cool and inviting down there. I noticed an iron ladder down the side of it, so I descended a couple of rungs. They seemed strong, so I went further. I'd only been there a moment," Stephen's voice shook a little. "When I heard Mary screeching my name."

"Screeching? That's a bit hard on her!"

"No. I *mean* screeching. I came back up. My head was going round a bit, I remember. Mary was *distraught*. She'd been calling me for ages, she said."

"So she'd come home early and caught you at it?" I could hear the smile in Tom's voice.

"No. That's the strange part. It was half past six. I must have been down there *three hours*."

"Three *hours*? Surely not. You must have misread the time when you went indoors."

"I said you wouldn't believe me!"

"True,"

"But I haven't told you everything. I checked my watch. It had stopped at three fourteen ... which would have been the time I went down the well."

Stephen's voice was definitely shaking now.

"How peculiar!" commented Tom.

"Very. But that's not all, either."

Stephen paused again; but whether for dramatic effect or from emotion it was hard to tell.

"Every clock in the house had also stopped. At *exactly* three fourteen."

Silence.

"That was strange, indeed."

I could imagine Tom clapping Stephen on the shoulder. I heard them move away. I'd been listening so intently that I jumped when I heard Myles' voice beside my ear.

"Ordering took ages," said he, reseating himself and picking up his tankard. "But the food shouldn't be long in coming." Myles loosened his tie and opened the collar of his shirt. "It's certainly cooler here in the shade. You chose the right table."

"I have an uncanny knack of knowing these things," I told him with a smile. "But what did you want to speak to me about?"

Myles hesitated before saying: "I wouldn't normally discuss a patient with anyone outside the practice ... but, since you're a solicitor, I'm sure you'll keep anything I tell you confidential?"

"Of course," I agreed absently, my mind still turning over the peculiar story I'd overheard. I watched the waitress bearing a tray towards us.

"A ploughman's and a chilli-con-carne," she announced. We accepted our respective meals and she swished away, her white apron accentuating the shapeliness of her bottom. I regarded my chilli-con-carne with great consternation. It was a very small portion—and I was ravenous.

"Anything the matter?" asked Myles.

"Absolutely nothing," I mumbled, my mouth full.

"I don't know how you can eat a hot meal like that on a day like this," Myles commented, tucking into his ploughman's lunch.

His meal did look good: crusty white bread, a whole pot of butter, a huge slice of cheddar cheese, a small mountain of salad, homemade chutney and pickled onions. It also looked bigger than mine. In fact, a great deal bigger.

"As I was saying," Myles swallowed a large mouthful of bread and cheese and took a swig of beer. "I would very much like you to meet a patient. Would you have a few minutes after lunch? She's the first of my afternoon calls."

I was longing for an afternoon's rest, so I didn't reply immediately.

Myles went on: "She's a lovely lady, you'll like her — and I'm sure she'll like you. She's terminally ill, you see, and she was asking me if I could suggest a solicitor to make a Will for her."

"Oh dear," I said. "How sad! How long …?"

"She has cancer," he said baldly. "She's had all the treatment the hospital can offer but she wanted to die in her own home. There's nothing more that can be done for her, medically speaking. I try to visit each day to make sure she's as comfortable and pain-free as possible." Myles kept his eyes down, applying himself with vigour to the plate in front of him.

"I see. Of course I'll come." What else could I say or do? "You say she wants to make a Will? I imagine she's on strong medication? If so, would you be able to certify that

SOLICITING FROM HOME

she's lucid and fully in possession of her senses?"

"'Compos mentis' you mean? Yes, I believe so. Would you need me to do that?"

"Shall we see whether she wants me to make a Will for her? I expect I'll get some idea of her mental state when I meet her. If she's obviously 'with it' I might ask you to be one of the witnesses. But I'm getting ahead of myself again. She hasn't even met me yet. She probably doesn't even know I exist."

"Oh yes, she knows all about you, of that I can assure you," he replied, looking mischievous. "It's the talk of the town that we have our own lady solicitor in Oldchurch now. Jennifer probably knows the colour of your hair and eyes, where you live, and the date the baby's due."

I blushed. The heat suffused my face from neck to hairline. If he noticed, Myles gave no sign.

He continued smoothly: "Her name is Jennifer Holloway. She used to sing professionally. Opera, mostly. She's been ill a long time, and, unfortunately, her family have fallen out with each other, and with her. She feels very much alone."

I finished my food and put down my knife and fork. The chilli had been delicious, but I was still hungry.

"How lucky I am to be young and expecting to bring new life into the world," I thought, "When Jennifer is preparing to go on a long solo journey." I felt the tears gathering behind my eyelids.

"Jennifer is not at all miserable. She's a formidable character. Just you wait and see," Myles said. "Now let's talk about something more cheerful."

Myles munched stolidly through his lunch while I chatted. Eventually, he wiped his mouth on a paper napkin and sighed. "I'm pretty full now. How about you? Is there anything else you would like?"

I had been waiting for this moment. "Yes," I said. "*Another* chilli-con-carne!"

His eyebrows shot up. "You're joking, surely?"

I shook my head.

"Are you sure you can fit another one in?"

I grinned. "I'm certain! After all, I am eating for two." Remembering my manners, I added: "Please."

When I'd finished my second chilli-con-carne the bowl was as clean as if I'd licked it. And I was ready, at last, to stagger the few yards up the street to where Jennifer lived.

But before we reach her door, I should just record that Tom told me Stephen's story first hand a few days later, asking for my help to find a meaning for this strange experience. Sporadically, over the course of the next two or three years, Stephen, Tom and I — sometimes together and at other times individually — consulted all sorts of records, books and documents. However, sad to tell, we never came close to finding an explanation.

- 10 -

Myles stopped in front of a door, its grey-blue paint grubby and chipped. Taking a key from his pocket, he inserted it into the lock and laid a finger to his lips, whispering: "Jennifer may be asleep. If she is, I try not to disturb her. We can always come back another time."

We crept up steep stairs to another door, which Myles opened a crack.

"There you are, my darling man!" Jennifer's voice was deep and husky. Myles opened the door fully and stepped into the room. I followed, leaving a space between us.

"And there you are, waiting for me, my dear Jennifer!" he responded. Crossing the floor to the bed, he took the white hand from the counterpane and pressed it to his lips.

The atmosphere was oppressive. An occasional flutter of the long, white muslin drapes drawn across the windows revealed that one of the sashes was open but the air did not penetrate far into the room.

I scanned the huge room from the doorway. Dim but not dark, and dominated by a wide brass bedstead, the room was filled to overflowing with objects. A beautifully embroidered silk shawl hung on the wall above the bed-head and a collection of antique snuffboxes graced the mantlepiece. Beneath the mantle, a Victorian fireplace was tiled in turquoise. The ceiling was white, its frieze picked out in a pale shade of green. The high walls, which were of a paler shade of turquoise than the fire tiles, were hung everywhere with pictures, behind which were lodged a profusion of photographs and theatre programmes.

"This is Melanie Russell," Myles introduced me. "She's the solicitor I mentioned. Melanie, this is my friend, Jennifer Holloway."

"How do you do?" I enquired formally, holding out my hand.

Dulled but beautiful blue eyes inspected me, their corners wrinkling up in a fleeting smile that matched the engaging one on her lips. Fine, very blonde hair fell in a fringe towards eyes set deeply into a sallow complexion. Her hand trembled as she lifted it from Myles' to brush mine.

"Not very well, actually," she replied. "But much better for seeing my dear Myles. And I'm very glad he brought you with him. There's something I need you to do for me."

That smile again.

"I'll be glad to help if I can," I murmured.

"I need to make a fresh Will. My family have written me off as a nuisance. Only strangers come to care for me now. I seldom see my sister and never see my husband." There was a catch in her voice as it weakened and grew more husky. "He can't bear illness, you see. He pays for a nurse to come in and a cleaner once a week. But he … he … I never see him."

"I'm sorry …" I faltered.

"It's all right, dear. Myles drops in most days and lifts my spirits with a song." I glanced at the doctor in surprise. He didn't notice because his back was turned as he pulled a chair closer to the bed, but Jennifer did.

SOLICITING FROM HOME

"I'll tell you about it all later, dear." Her eyes rested on Myles for a split second. "There's only one person who deserves to have any of my money. Will you come back soon so that I can get this all off my chest and die peacefully?" She patted my hand as I seated myself in the chair beside her bed.

"Of course," I agreed, feeling her hand's coldness. I covered it with mine and willed strength and vitality into her.

"Maybe tomorrow?" she suggested. "I'm at my best in the morning."

I opened my mental diary. "Yes, that will be fine. Shall we make it eleven thirty?"

"Thank you," she nodded in acceptance. "My nurse will have been by then. I should at least be presentable."

"I will need the names and addresses of two executors. And the full names and addresses of your beneficiaries," I told her. "And — should your first choice of beneficiary die before you — do think about whom else you would like to benefit from your Will instead."

"I understand," she said. "But that's most unlikely."

"I know, but the most important thing is that you do exactly as *you* want with your money. It's best to provide for every contingency."

"Good. That's settled then." Jennifer looked relieved but there was the suspicion of a tear in the corner of her eye. She took her hand away from me and gave it instead to Myles. He smiled at her.

"Will you sing for me, now?" she whispered, looking up at him affectionately.

"Only if you will sing with me. A duet?" he suggested. "What about 'Somewhere'?" And without waiting for her reply he launched into the song from West Side Story. "There's a …"

"… place for us," she sang.

Their voices rose and fell together in perfect synchrony and harmony; his, a mellow baritone, and hers, a deep, rich contralto at which her speaking voice had merely hinted. I sat there, spellbound by the beauty of it; the two voices interweaving with natural perfection in that darkened sickroom, transporting us all to another place 'somewhere'. When they finished she was breathless, but her eyes were sparkling and she was smiling.

"Bravo!" I cried clapping, regardless of the tears making tracks down my cheeks. "More!"

"That's enough for me," sighed Jennifer. "Myles, sing 'Volare' for me?"

"Volare it is," he said, striking a pose at the foot of the bed. His voice soared into the Italian song, reverberating in waves of captivating sound, raising the vibration in the room and enchanting both of his listeners.

"More!" I heard myself demand when the last note had died away and I was able to speak. Without further encouragement, he sang 'O Sole Mio'. We listened, enraptured.

As the last note faded, Myles looked at his watch. "Jennifer, I must fly! I'll pop in tomorrow afternoon to make sure Melanie hasn't tired you out."

He kissed her hand at parting and with a brief "Goodbye till then," made for the stairs.

SOLICITING FROM HOME

"Thank you for that wonderful treat," I said, trying to swallow my emotion. "I'll look forward to seeing you tomorrow."

I squeezed her hand in farewell and followed her doctor down the stairs.

"Sorry about that, Melanie. I find I have to go quickly or I'd never be allowed to stop singing."

"I gathered that! I have to go, too. I must put my feet up while I can. My doctor says so. But there's something I need to say. Do you have time?"

"Yes, of course," he answered. "I have to take the car for my next call. Let me give you a lift home and we can chat on the way."

Ryan would have known the make of Myles' car but I did not: suffice it to say it was a huge brute of a silver-grey sports car and that the dashboard was walnut-veneered around an array of dials and switches. He had left it in full sunshine with the hood down and the grey leather passenger seat was hot on my posterior.

We accelerated up the High Street to Rose Cottage and my spirits lifted as my hair blew back. Myles drew the car into the kerb. Wonderfully enlivened, I said: "Thank you, Myles! For lunch, a client and most of all for the wonderful songs."

"I'm glad you feel better," he responded with a smile. "What did you want to say to me?"

"It seems pretty clear to me that Jennifer wants to make you a beneficiary of her Will. That could be difficult for you if her family argued 'undue influence'. In other words, that you'd put pressure on her to make her Will in your favour."

"Yes, I know," he replied seriously. "I also know how shabbily she has been treated by her family — apart from one sister — since she's been terminally ill. She tells me her husband has practically deserted her now that she has very little money left. I only want her to die happy that she's arranged everything as she wants it."

"Very commendable," I applauded. "But there's another problem. If I ask you to witness the Will — which I will need to do to make it clear that she is of 'right mind', to use the legal jargon — any gift to you will be invalidated."

"Phew!" Myles let out a long breath. "That's actually a really good thing. Jennifer will think she's done what she needs to do. I witness her Will. I can't take any benefit. And the result is … er …what *is* the result, Melanie?"

"If she's made some alternative arrangements, the bequest to you would pass down to the next level of beneficiaries." I paused.

"And if not?" he prompted. "What then?"

"Then the Intestacy Rules would apply. The problem there is that they're complicated. Most of her investments and belongings would probably go to her husband, but not necessarily all of them."

"Well, that's good, too. You only have to make sure that she states alternative beneficiaries and then we're all happy."

"I'll do my best," I confirmed. "I'm really glad I hitched a ride but I mustn't keep you."

I began to struggle out of the low-slung sports car but Myles was there instantly. He opened the car door for me,

SOLICITING FROM HOME

put a hand under my elbow and hoisted me out of his gleaming monster of a machine.

"Now — rest!" he ordered. And I was glad to obey.

When I arrived at Jennifer's door the next morning, I was a minute or two late for our appointment. The door was ajar. I knocked but there was no answer. I waited for the length of a dozen heartbeats and knocked again. No response. I pushed the door open and called. Still no reply. I tried again.

"Hello? Jennifer? It's Melanie. I'm sorry I'm a few minutes late." Still no response. I'd started up the stairs but now stopped to listen. I could hear nothing. Not a single sound.

'Strange,' I thought as I continued to mount the stairs slowly. 'Maybe she's in the bathroom.'

The thought was embarrassing. My heart was beating strangely, racing more than my slow ascent of the stairs warranted. A dread that I would find her dead crept over me like a cold mist. Fear loomed in the quality of the silence, as though all feeling, all light and noise had been extinguished. Movement was difficult, slow and deliberate, my feet feeling as if I were walking without gravity. It seemed ages before I reached the door to her room although it couldn't have been more than a few moments. The door was shut. I knocked tentatively and tried again:

"Hello? Jennifer? It's Melanie."

Still no answer. Slowly turning the handle, I opened the door. Jennifer was sitting up in bed in a colourfully embroidered silk bed-jacket. She turned her beautiful smile on me.

"Hello Melanie. How considerate of you to creep up the stairs. I didn't hear a sound."

"I did knock ..."

"Did you, dear? Are you sure? I fear I must be getting deaf. Never mind, you're here now. Come over here and sit on the bed." She patted it invitingly.

I went over to the bed, but pulled up a chair to seat myself. "I'm sorry I'm late," I apologised.

"You're not late at all, Melanie." Jennifer reached over and took my hand. "Just breathe deeply, my dear. Why, your hand is icy. You look very pale — as if you'd seen a ghost."

I took a deep breath and smiled. It was I who should have been comforting her. "I'm fine, Jennifer. Thank you for your concern. It was just ..."

I was not sure how to continue, but Jennifer's eyes looked shrewdly into mine. "Ah, I see. You thought I might be dead."

It was a bald statement, but so true. I was horrified she had guessed my feelings so accurately, but could not deny that she was right.

"Yes," I said. "I *was* apprehensive."

"I know, dear. I *know*." I was at a loss for words but Jennifer's smile lit up her face again. "It's so good to hear someone admit that. Everyone who comes to see me tries to cheer me up by telling me I look well, that I have plenty of time, that I'm going to get better. We all know that's not true — and it's hurtful that there is no honesty between us. Worse, in fact. We know it's a lie and yet we try to protect each other from the truth." Her voice was weakening. She took a quivering breath and whispered: "Only you had the courage to admit your fears. That has been a great gift to me. Thank you."

Her beautiful eyes were glistening with tears and I felt mine brimming, too. She took my hand and gave it a quick squeeze. The effort of speaking had obviously tired her because she closed her eyes and let her head fall back against the pillow. Not knowing quite what to do, I simply held her hand in mine and gently stroked the back of it. No words could express my feelings, so I stayed quiet and the silence lengthened between us, the only sound the companionable ticking of her bedside clock.

Eventually, Jennifer's chest heaved uncomfortably in a great sigh and then she spoke again, her voice stronger although her eyes stayed closed.

"Until you are close to death yourself, you never realise how good it is to be able to speak freely. Even about death. *Especially* about death. I want to talk about dying. Tell someone how it feels. Explain what my fears are. I only need someone to listen. And then I need to talk about what will happen, about how I will die, what I want to happen afterwards. Instead you have to comfort those who come to visit you. They would be much happier if you would conveniently creep away and die alone — or unnoticed in a hospital bed amongst clanging bedpans."

I knew this was all too true. Even in my short experience as a solicitor I had attended people dying in hospital when they knew that they would have to make some legal arrangements for their assets.

I felt a warm tear edge out of the corner of my left eye and wiped it away with my free hand, grateful that Jennifer's eyes were still closed.

"I think it's just that people don't know what to do when someone is dying," I said. "They can't cope. They're not taught. It seems to me that society generally is happier denying that anyone ever dies. Even I can see that life and youth are worshipped these days."

"I know. You're right. I shouldn't expect more of them than they can give."

"No. You have every right to speak openly. After all, death comes to all of us, even if we don't care to think about it — or even to acknowledge it."

"It's not as though I *want* to die. Far from it. But I would like to cry about the fact that I *am* on the way out. I want someone to hold my hand as you are now and tell me it's all right. That death is okay. Not something to be avoided at all costs. Not that dying is my *fault*."

"It's not your fault," I told her. "As my mother would say: 'When God calls we cannot disobey.'" A slight pressure on my hand encouraged me. I had no idea whether I was saying the right thing, but now that I'd started I couldn't help myself. I carried on. "A long time ago, I was looking through the Bible my mother kept on her bedside table. I came upon a note addressed to me. I read it, of course. She had written it for me to find — but not until after her death. It said: 'Forgive me for leaving you, my darling, but when God calls we cannot disobey.' I put the note back where I'd found it and cried buckets! Then I had to pretend I hadn't seen it. I've never told her. But I've never forgotten those words."

Jennifer opened her eyes. "No, I can see you haven't. Do you believe in God?" Not the usual question from a client to a solicitor. How could I answer honestly?

SOLICITING FROM HOME

"I think so. I believe in a Creator. And a Force for great good that decides our destiny. Do *you* believe in God?"

"Yes," she said quietly. "I think perhaps I do."

"I find comfort in going to church. And praying always helps me in both good times and bad," I said. "My mother has been ill for a long time but she always says that you are never given more pain than you can bear, and she is seldom downcast. And as for money — she believes that the Lord always provides. And he does! Even when my parents had to leave everything behind in Burma and start again after World War Two. But enough of me! What can I do for you?"

"You've already done more than you know," she said, with a whimsical half-smile. "I like your mother's wisdom. Is she afraid of death?"

"Actually, she says she's quite looking forward to it. She has almost died twice — once on the operating table and once when she was very ill from septicaemia — and she says the experience was wonderful each time."

"What was it like?"

"Apparently she found herself looking down on her body from above, watching the nursing staff fighting to save her. She felt nothing but peace. Soon she realised she was moving, travelling along a tunnel of white light into a warm, bright space of overwhelming love. Her mother, and other loved ones who had gone before, were waiting for her."

"That sounds wonderfully reassuring."

"I know. I find it so, too. She says she will never forget feeling surrounded by the amazing power of love. Time had no meaning. She wanted to rest there forever. But her mother explained that it wasn't her time and next minute she was drawn back into her body with a jolt. She said it was a shock and, at first, she didn't want to return. But I'm glad to say that she's reconciled to being here now — and she's very excited about this baby of mine."

"New life," Jennifer sighed and I cursed my tongue. But then she smiled. "How good to know that life carries on. I may be on the way out, but your baby is nearly ready to come in."

I put a hand down to hide the baby's sudden kick, but Jennifer had noticed. "Do you mind?" She stretched her hand towards me.

"Not at all." She rested her hand on my moving abdomen and her smile widened. "Thank you. Would you mind making a cup of tea for us before we get down to business?"

I found the kitchen, the kettle, the teapot, the tea, mugs and some milk and before long we were sitting together like old friends gossiping over a cuppa as I took instructions for her Will and for a Power of Attorney, checking her family arrangements and giving her appropriate advice.

By the time Jennifer had considered my legal advice and made the decisions required of her, she could hardly keep her eyes open.

"I must leave you to rest now. Myles warned me he would drop in this afternoon to make sure that I hadn't tired you too much. So unless I want to be in his bad books, I must go. But let me make you comfortable first. Is there anything you need?"

"Thank you," she said after I had rearranged her pillows, removed her bed jacket and supplied a glass of water. "I *am* tired. I'll sleep now. Close the door downstairs, please." She closed her eyes.

"Of course," I assured her. "I'll be in touch soon. I know you need these things as soon as possible. Sleep well."

She seemed to be asleep already. I straightened the bed cover and left.

The following morning I set off up the High Street once again, leaving my trusty Poppadum to guard the house from intruders.

The evening before, I had been delighted to find that my creative juices had flowed so well and so fast that I had completed the drafts of Jennifer's Power of Attorney and of her Will much more quickly than I anticipated. I peeped into the sitting room to find Ryan mesmerised by the television so I decided to carry on and prepare the engrossments. For once, the old typewriter had co-operated and within a couple of hours the engrossments were ready for Jennifer's signature.

Ryan brought a cup of tea up to me and found me sewing the Will together with black tape. Poppadum was curled up on the floor beside me.

He looked incredulously at what I was doing.

"I'm just sewing this Will together," I remarked.

"*Sewing?*"

"As you see." I was enjoying teasing him.

"Why on earth are you sewing it? Can't you use staples or eyelets or something?"

"I didn't have enough of that special Will paper. I've had to type it on separate sheets of foolscap engrossment paper. And that means it has to be *sewn* together."

"But I thought you said it all had to be on one sheet of paper."

"You're quite right. That's the best way for any document, especially for Wills. But if that's not possible, you can sew the document up like this." I waved the big-eyed needle threaded with narrow black tape. "The thing I *must* remember now is to make sure that the testator — or rather, this time, the testatrix — and the witnesses *all* sign their names on *each* page of the Will."

"I suppose you're going to tell me that's because you're not supposed to attach anything to a Will?" Ryan suggested.

"So you *were* listening!"

"Of course, I listen to every word that drops from your dewy lips!"

"Flatterer! Now, do you know why I'm using *black* tape?"

"To sew it up?"

"Idiot." I chided fondly. "Yes, of *course*. But why not red tape?"

"Why do I have a feeling that you're going to tell me?"

"Probably because I am! It's a convention in the legal profession. Black for Wills; green for Agreements and other non-litigious documents; and red for Court documents and for binding up bundles of papers."

"So that's where the saying 'too much red tape' comes from! I might have guessed lawyers were involved somewhere," Ryan teased.

I slipped the needle from the tape and tied the traditional double knot in the middle of the front sheet.

"There. Doesn't that look neat?" I asked, admiring my

SOLICITING FROM HOME

handiwork.

"Indeed it does," he agreed. "You had just the right amount of tape. Very clever."

"That's because I measured it," I said. "Two and a half times the length between the first and last holes."

"Holes?"

"Yes, I made them first, with the needle. Five holes about half an inch in from the side edge. The first in the middle, the next two holes about an inch in from the top and bottom of the page, and the other two equally spaced between. Then it's just a case of ordinary back stitch, starting from the middle and …"

"Very clev …"

"I suppose it's more like a version of blanket stitch," I reflected, holding the document up the better to inspect the stitches that were oversewn along its length.

"Quite possibly, darl. Now, tell me — have you finished your endeavours for tonight?"

"Yes, it's definitely time for bed," I admitted, carefully stowing the Will and Power of Attorney away in a folder.

And so it was with some pride that I set forth with my briefcase tucked under my arm into yet another warm and beautiful morning. The High Street was busy and it seemed that everyone I passed was as happy as I. Women smiled at me generously and men raised or touched their hats with a murmured 'Good Morning'.

Jennifer's door was ajar again. On this particular lovely morning, however, there was no air of sadness or foreboding. I had a presentiment that Myles would be there, and, sure enough, I heard his voice upraised in song as I set foot on the stair. I paused long enough for him to finish his rendering of 'Dear Lord and Father of Mankind' before I entered.

This time he was seated on the bed, holding her hand; Jennifer was lying back against the pillows, her face pale and her eyes closed. She was very still and for a moment I thought she had already passed away. Then her eyelids fluttered softly and her chest rose a fraction.

Myles looked at me and slowly shook his head, pressing a finger to his lips. Tears pricked my eyes and I began to retreat as silently as I could. Jennifer must have heard me, for her head turned towards me, her eyes slowly opened and her hand moved convulsively on the sheet.

Blinking the tears away, I drew closer and stood on the other side of the bed from Myles. Jennifer's lips twitched. She put her hand on her chest and slowed her breathing. With what seemed a stupendous effort she whispered:

"Have you brought it?"

I nodded, withdrawing the Will from my thin briefcase.

"I just need to read it through to you, Jennifer, to make sure it's what you want. Is that all right?"

Her lips twitched into a half smile; she mouthed 'yes' though no sound came out. I sat on the bed and took her hand in mine.

"You don't have to speak. Squeeze my hand if there's anything you don't understand,"

The Will was short; it did not take long to read it out loud. I was very pleased that I had managed to take her rambling instructions and distil them into three pages of foolscap. Jennifer appeared to be concentrating but the hand I held stayed still.

"Squeeze if everything is as you wanted your Will to be." I felt the soft pressure of her fingers. I looked at Myles, questioningly. I wanted to ensure that he had noticed. He nodded and reached into his medical bag.

"I have a pen here," he said, passing it to me. "Jennifer, my dear, let me support you while I put this cushion in your back. There. Now you can sign more easily."

Before I gave the pen to Jennifer, I checked the ink in it was blue, so that the original Will would be simply identifiable, since the photocopies of it that would later be required would show the signatures as black. I held the Will firmly on top of my briefcase and offered it to her.

"I need one signature, here," I pointed. "However you normally sign a cheque." She laboriously signed her name. Her signature was full of flourishes. "Only two more, now. Here ... and here. Don't worry, I'll date it and Myles and I have most of the writing to do."

I showed her where to sign at the top of each of the other pages of her Will. When she had finished I thanked her, quickly dated it and added my signature, name, address and occupation at the end of the Will. Then I added my signature below hers on its other two pages. I passed the document to Myles and he did the same before handing it back to me.

"There," I said, more briskly than I intended because I was keeping my tears at bay. "That's all done, now. You don't need to worry about it any more."

A beautiful smile lit up Jennifer's face. Pulling Myles closer, she whispered something in his ear. His lips sketched a sad half smile as he raised his eyes towards the ceiling and his rich voice once more rang out in an emotional rendition of 'O Sole Mio'.

I watched as her smile broadened and then froze. A small choking noise came from her throat. Her eyes widened and grew still, staring unseeing at the ceiling.

Myles' voice broke. His eyelashes hid his eyes as he drew her fingers to his lips. Gently replacing her hand on the coverlet, he placed two fingers against her throat, feeling for a pulse. Finding none, he shook his head with a sad smile. He closed her eyelids with his fingertips, bending his head as if in prayer. I bent my head, too and the words of the Lord's Prayer whispered themselves through my lips.

We stood then and it was natural to move together. Myles put his arm round me in a one-armed hug.

It was only then that I remembered the Power of Attorney. No matter that she had not signed it, the document was quite redundant now.

- 11 -

Soon a succession of clients found their way to my house. Most of them required Wills and I was very happy to oblige, not least because I knew I was supplying a necessary service. That wasn't the only reason of course. I had wanted to be a stay-at-home wife and mother for as long as I could remember, but Ryan and I had had several long discussions after Mr Standish had made his suggestion to me that Oldchurch was in need of a solicitor.

I had realised that I would miss my work and we both knew that it would be very helpful for me to earn some money to put in to the family coffers, so in the end Ryan and I had decided that, with Mr Standish trying so hard to help me, I would try setting up my own practice and working from home — but not until the baby was at least six months old. I wanted to have time to settle into being a mother.

I still had roughly a month before the baby was due to make an appearance and the plan was that I would use this time to prepare for the baby's arrival.

Although we knew there was a lot to organise to set up in practice, we both thought there would be plenty of time to start the business from scratch after the baby was born. I began to make a list of organisations with which I needed to register and was a little daunted by the number. I put that list to one side and started another. This one was of connections to local businesses and clubs, because, since I was forbidden by the Solicitors' Practice Rules from advertising, word of mouth was the form of publicity on which I would need to rely most.

In the event, however, there was very little time for me to do any of these things at all, and certainly not in the methodical manner I had planned. Mr Standish kept me very busy indeed. Scarcely a day went by without new clients beating their way to my door. I seemed to be the latest fashion: word of my existence and legal services ran round the town a great deal faster than I could walk.

I loved meeting new people, putting them at their ease and doing my best to give good legal advice. That was the easy, enjoyable part. It was after clients left me that my work started in earnest, whether it was telephoning on their behalf, drafting documents or writing legal letters. Generally speaking, a single client's instructions would take me a day or more to complete, but that day's work would not all be done in one shift, the hours would usually be spread over several days while I waited for responses or written replies, or the amendment or approval of draft documents.

The weeks flew past in an orgy of work intermingled with preparations for the birth and the formal opening of my practice. Mr Standish was amazingly helpful. True to his word, he recommended me to a delightful woman named Olive who was a few years older than me and a registered baby-minder, but more importantly she had several well-behaved, charming children of her own. I came to rely on her good sense and pragmatic humour to keep me from panicking in the few weeks before my baby was born. Afterwards, she was a fount of knowledge and a reliable comfort and friend. However, our first meeting was not without an initial bristliness.

We met on the day I signed the overdraft documentation

SOLICITING FROM HOME

in Mr Standish's office. As soon as the business had been completed, Mr Standish pushed his chair back from his desk and came round to stand in front of me.

"Now my dear," he said, his eyes twinkling in their trademark manner, as he rested back against his desk.. "I have arranged to take you to meet another customer of mine who will make an excellent baby minder."

"But I'm not ready," I protested.

Mr Standish was having none of it. "You'll need one when you set up your practice," he insisted. "And I've already told Mrs Jenkins that I will take you round to introduce you." He glanced at his watch and continued: "In fact, we're likely to be late unless we go now."

Realising that protest was useless, I heaved myself to my feet. Mr Standish gave me his arm and we waddled along the street together at the slow pace dictated by my girth, lack of breath and the heat of the day.

Mrs Jenkins lived in a modern detached house in a lane that ran between the two main streets of the town. The neatly painted house was surrounded by a garden full of flowers and a lawn scuffed by children's feet, and I was soon to discover that the back garden was festooned with play equipment, including swings, slides and a paddling pool.

Mr Standish escorted me to the front door, introduced me to Olive and left. I found direct blue eyes searching mine.

"You'd better come in," she said, standing aside for me to enter. As soon as I did, I was aware of a warm family atmosphere and the smell of home-baked bread. I sniffed appreciatively.

Olive smiled over her shoulder as she led me down a short passage to the sitting room.

"I've made my own ever since the bread strike a few years ago," she said, and I felt an instant bond as my father had started making bread at the same time and still did so every week.

The sitting room was a comfortable place furnished with sofas and easy chairs and a number of ornaments. Olive saw me taking this in.

"I never move anything for the children I look after. They soon learn not to touch. You only have to tell them a couple of times."

This was what I wanted to hear. Friends of mine with small children insisted that it was necessary to remove all breakable objects from their vicinity — but then they allowed their children to touch and hold anything they wanted, even if it meant bringing an object down from a place where it was out of reach.

"I presume that's all right with you?"

I realised that my thoughts had been unspoken. "Oh, yes!" I agreed. "Just how I intend it to be at home."

Olive was looking me up and down. I felt uncomfortable under her scrutiny, but before I could say anything she blurted: "Don't you think you should *have* the baby *before* you think about leaving it with someone else?"

I felt wrong-footed, mostly because I had been thinking much the same myself. I had just lowered myself onto the sofa and so found myself looking up at her.

"I know, I thought that too. But Mr Standish insisted ..."

"Well," she said. "You're the one having the baby. Not Mr Standish."

Astonished, I could think of nothing to say. She was right, of course. It was my baby and that had nothing whatsoever to do with Mr. Standish. Why, then, had I acquiesced so easily to his plans? My original intentions had been swept away by Mr Standish's dynamism. I supposed it was because he was a man. And a man in a position of some authority who expected me to gratefully do as he suggested. There was still, in the nineteen seventies, some unwritten rule that young women obeyed older men, particularly those with an air of authority. Not me! I thought. I'm an independent woman.

"You're right!" I said, and pushed myself to my feet. "I'll wait until the baby's born. May I come back then?"

Olive's face had broken into a grin. "That's my girl! I like a woman with spirit. And yes, of course you can."

"Thank you. Until then, then." I smiled and made for the door, but Olive's stiff manner relented.

"Since you're here, you might as well look round," she said, with a half smile on her lips and a real smile in her eyes. "Ask any questions you have. I'll do my best to answer."

That was the beginning of a wonderful friendship that supported me through tough times and I hope that I did the same for her. It did not take long for me to register that she had exactly the attitude to children — loving but firm, with definite boundaries — that I intended to have with mine. The house was spotless and she cooked each day for children and adults alike.

"Obviously, you'll breast feed," she said. "But when it comes to weaning, I find it best to put the same food I feed the others through a sieve. Children learn to eat everything that way." She saw my shocked expression and laughed. "Not all at once! I take it easily, first a little fruit. A few weeks later some vegetables. Wait and see! I'll educate you in the way of it."

We parted on the best of terms — the mature woman with the wide smile, ample bosom, clear blue eyes and wonderful skin and the heavily pregnant, hot, sweaty younger woman. I knew I would go back to visit her and show her my newborn, even if I decided that I would look after the baby myself and had no need of a baby-minder.

It was good to realise that I — and not Ryan or Mr Standish — could make this decision on my own. It gave me a certain feeling of power over my own destiny and that of my child. That said, I had little doubt that when I returned to see Olive I would ask her to take care of the child for some part of the day while I worked. I enjoyed my work so much. I knew I made a difference to people's lives by guiding them through tough times and legal procedures, and that I would not be satisfied to be at home all day with a baby. I assured myself it would be a waste of my education, skills and abilities.

I was in high spirits as I walked home. If my weight had allowed, I would have skipped with excitement, but in my current condition I had no alternative but to waddle. So waddle home I did, drew myself a glassful of cool water and retired to my bed for a welcome afternoon rest. Paperwork and cooking supper could wait.

As I grew heavier and the baby took up even more of the available space in my abdomen, I became much more tired. The weather grew hotter still and more enervating. Sometimes I prayed for a thunderstorm to clear the air, but my prayers went unanswered, although all hopes I might have nurtured about finding work were soon more than

SOLICITING FROM HOME

fulfilled.

Mr and Mrs White were thrilled that I had managed to make their Wills so rapidly and passed my name on to several friends so that, even without Mr Standish's sterling efforts, I would have been busy.

But just after I'd made the Wills for the Whites, Mrs Kendall had entered my life with all the accompanying drama I have mentioned. She too, sang my praises, and before long I had several people asking me to act for them in connection with conveyancing matters. Sadly, I had to refuse these requests as I simply did not have the resources.

Instead, I stuck to making Wills until I thought I would be able to advise people in my sleep. I was almost convinced that I could draft a Will accurately in my sleep, too. The problem was that I had to be awake to give the advice and also to do the typing — and with my increasing girth the distance between me and the table on which the typewriter was perched was growing, too. I could neither sit nor stand comfortably for long and my sleep was disturbed with discomfort. Eventually, I had to admit to myself, Ryan, Mr Standish and my clients that I could take no more clients for the present. I would complete the Wills I had promised to a particularly beige-looking couple, appropriately named Mr and Mrs Brown. Then I would take a rest.

Both Ryan and Mr Standish were understanding and co-operative. It was one less worry when I realised I need not be anxious about their disfavour. But the Wills seemed to take forever to complete. I was clumsy; I was hot; I was sweaty. Nothing was easy. When I pulled the engrossment of the second Will from the typewriter and checked it to find it was mistake-free — the last of four attempts — I could have cried with relief. Instead, I telephoned my clients and made an appointment for them to call in the following morning to sign their Wills. Now I could indulge myself and take a cool bath.

The bath was bliss, even though there was so much of me that I misjudged the amount of water and it was soon slopping over the edge. I simply didn't care since at last I was wallowing in coolness.

Then the pains began. First, a sharp pain somewhere deep inside that made me gasp, but soon they were coming fast, stabbing until it seemed I was awash with pain. There was neither time nor space to breathe. I found myself panting. I tried to heave myself out of the bath, but my strength deserted me.

I was stuck. I was scared. Would I ever get out of the bath? I was really frightened that, if the baby came fast, it would drown before it took breath.

Panic set in. I had no idea of the time. When would Ryan be home? I needed him. I needed him NOW!

The bathroom door was shut, but I could hear Poppadum scratching at it, howling. Owowowowoooo! wowowowooooo!

Then suddenly she stopped, I heard her claws on the floor and: "Melanie? Melanie! Where are you? Get off, you stupid dog! Melanie?"

Never had I been so glad to hear his voice — and that was saying a great deal since I loved him so much.

Relief flooded through me. I managed to croak "I'm here!" But by then, Poppadum had pushed past Ryan into the bathroom, and tried to get into the bath with me. He dragged her off. Having taken one look at me and thrown

SOLICITING FROM HOME

his briefcase down, loosened his tie — all in one swift movement — he was on his knees beside me.

"Is it...?" He grabbed my hand and clung to it. "Is it the baby?" Ryan was white. He looked as scared as I felt.

I squeezed his hand hard, noticing that my knuckles were white. But I made no sound. Instead, I nodded, biting my lip to prevent myself from screaming. A scream was building deep inside me. Only that primeval sound would bear the baby into the world on its wings. I stopped 'being British' and let the scream rip — and with it I felt my waters burst.

Ryan pulled the plug out of the bath, ran to the telephone, and called the mid-wife. He came back to me and somehow managed to haul me out of the bath but I could not move further than the floor.

By the time the midwife arrived, some ten minutes later, Ryan was sitting on the floor supporting a towel-draped wife in the second stage of labour.

The midwife took over and it wasn't long before the birthing was finished.

"You have a lovely baby girl, Mrs Russell," she smiled, wrapping the baby in a towel and handing her to me to hold.

Although Ryan had been relieved to leave the midwife in charge, he confessed to me later that he wished he'd been there when Sarah-Jane finally saw the light of day. Unfortunately the room was too cramped for more than two people and he'd been banished to the sitting room to march up and down in time-honoured new father fashion. When Sarah-Jane was finally ready for his inspection, carried in the arms of the mid-wife, her father was out on the patio smoking a cigarette.

Not long afterwards, when Ryan had washed his hands and received a lecture on the evils of smoking, the midwife took her leave, promising to call in the following day to check on our progress. She left with a sentimental smile at our little family as we indulged in a cuddle on the sofa.

The rest of that evening passed in a flash. I was on cloud nine, adrenalin from the sudden, easy birth rushing round my body so that I couldn't help smiling despite my soreness. My baby was so perfect, so sweet, and made such delightful little mumbling sounds that I fell in love with her instantly. All I wanted was to show her off: and before long Ryan had phoned my parents and invited them to come over for that precise purpose.

They were delighted to oblige, arriving within half an hour, still quarrelling about the speed of my father's driving. Some things never changed.

The night had been surreal. I had been sent upstairs with Sarah-Jane to rest while down below, new father, new grandparents and several neighbours had gathered in a noisy celebration fuelled by champagne. I tossed and turned, trying to sleep. My little baby was wrapped in new clothes, swathed in a new shawl and ensconced in her baby basket beside me on the double bed.

I felt incredibly lonely. She had been part of me for so long, and I had loved her every movement inside me, longed to see her — and yet, now, I was filled with emptiness. A happy emptiness, but still an emptiness. I longed to hold her and wondered if it were permitted. The midwife had impressed on me that we would both need rest and sleep and my mother had endorsed this stricture. But

SOLICITING FROM HOME

no-one was near now.

I could bear it no longer. I heaved myself over, raised myself on an elbow and pulled the basket towards me. I found myself looking into deep baby blue eyes and my heart yearned for her. To hell with people who thought they knew best! She was my daughter: I was her mother! And I wanted her close to me, in my arms, not twelve inches away encased in material and imprisoned in a basket. Her eyes had closed, her eyelids swollen by her sudden entrance into the world, but her tiny sighing breaths were ancient magic. She was an old soul, born already knowledgeable and full of wisdom. But she was also, simply and completely, my baby.

I cannot describe the immense joy, total happiness and unconditional love that enveloped the two of us a few moments later, when I had undressed her and pressed her unimaginable softness to my naked skin. She was blood of my blood, skin of my skin, bone of my bone — and the joyous intensity of love that bound us was so deep it bordered between the slicing pain of childbirth and the ecstasy of orgasm.

So consuming was this passion, that any wish I had to be present at the feasting in the room below dissolved instantly. My baby and I were sufficient unto ourselves. I could not bear the thought of sleeping. This overwhelming, immense, enthralling love demanded to be experienced forever; I must stay awake lest it faded.

But of course, when my parents came to say goodbye, they found us both contentedly asleep; so they left us curled up together, crept down the stairs and drove away.

I half-woke when Ryan joined us, conscious of his weight on the mattress and the heaviness of the arm he flung around us, but slipped back into sleep on a wave of utter contentment.

I drifted back to consciousness to the sound of a baby crying and it took me a moment or two to realise it was mine. My real live baby. I vaguely remembered floating off to sleep with her in my arms. Sudden realisation dawned that she was no longer near me. Where was she? I was fully awake instantly, beginning to panic. Where was she? Close to me. She must be close because the noise was deafening! I found her back in her basket. Ryan must have removed her from my arms and installed her there, but what to do now? Feed her? No-one had given me lessons! How could I do it? I chided myself for being silly and let my innate instinct take over from my panicking brain. I sat up and put her to my breast. Instant peace.

A few moments later, Ryan opened the door and stood there gazing at us with a silly bewitched smile on his face.

"I've got the day off," he said.

The doorbell rang, shattering the moment into a million and one pieces. Ryan and I gazed at each other open-mouthed, each knowing what the other was feeling. Neither of us wanted to venture downstairs, even for congratulations: we wanted a little time together to enjoy the miracle we had achieved: a baby who was part of us and would join us together forever.

The doorbell rang again.

"Who on earth?" Ryan asked, his mouth setting in a firm line.

Memory rushed back. I gasped.

"Of course! Mr and Mrs Brown!"

"What? Who the hell are they?"

SOLICITING FROM HOME

"Clients of mine! I arranged for them to come and sign their Wills today."

"Whaaaaat??"

"Before my bath. Before things ... happened." I started to giggle and found it impossible to stop.

Ryan threw me a puzzled glance and galloped downstairs, taking them at least two at a time. I could hear his thumping footsteps across the sitting room and then the front door being thrown open. A short muffled conversation ensued, first Ryan's low tones, then a feminine cry of exclamation followed by an earnest exchange of words. Next, I heard three sets of steps into the room below and the closing of the door. Ryan's footsteps on the stairs: then his head appearing round the door.

"They say ..."

"I know. It's urgent. Throw me my negligée, would you?"

"This thing?" He caught up the frothy confection that hung behind the door, a special gift from Ryan when he'd heard I was pregnant. I'd been saving it to wear to lend me a little glamour after the birth: now was the time!

"Thanks. And a hairbrush?"

He grabbed the brush and a hand mirror from the dressing table and passed them both to me.

"Won't you need the Wills?"

"Yes, of course! They're over there in the file by the typewriter. Can you get me a tray and a pen with blue ink?" I was already wrapped in the negligee and was busy brushing my hair into some semblance of tidiness. "And when you come back, can you bring the Browns with you? I'll need you to stay and be a witness."

He was gone before I could say 'knife'. While he rummaged around downstairs for the items I'd requested, I checked my appearance in the mirror, surprised to find that I looked radiant. My eyes, skin and hair shining with happiness, I looked prettier than I had ever done before. Delighted with myself on all counts, I sat back and prepared to meet my clients.

Mr and Mrs Brown were very grateful that I'd agreed to see them, made all the right comments about Sarah-Jane's beauty, her father's brains and my happiness, and promised that they would be gone as soon as the Wills were signed.

They were as good as their word and left soon afterwards, leaving Ryan and me slightly fazed but very happy.

"That can't happen very often," Ryan remarked. "Not many solicitors would see their clients within twelve hours of giving birth!"

"Not many solicitors give birth!" I trumped. "Though I think there will be more of us — women solicitors, that is — in the future." My words were prophetic. Within thirty years, more than half the number of students qualifying as solicitors would be women.

"Okay, solicitor-who-has-given-birth, I'm famished! Are you? I can rustle up some eggs and bacon, if you like."

"You're an angel. Yes please."

We had scarcely finished our breakfast when the midwife called to show me the knack of breastfeeding, bathing and nappy-changing; and soon after she left a procession of people started to arrive, variously bearing good wishes, flowers, champagne and baby clothes. Olive brought a steak casserole, an apple pie and a couple of

SOLICITING FROM HOME

bottles of stout for me. She declared that stout, being full of iron, was particularly good for breastfeeding mothers and insisted that I drank some there and then.

My parents returned too, bearing more food and a small bag full of my mother's clothes. "Since you didn't make it to hospital, I'm here to look after you," she declared. "Someone has to make sure you rest."

I basked in all the attention, congratulations and assistance for a couple of days, but two days later the baby blues set in and I started crying for no reason. I'd just about mastered how to deal with a small baby by that time, but my mother insisted on staying to help with all the chores and for moral support since Ryan had already returned to work.

"You need something to occupy your mind, darling," she suggested. "Is there any work you can do?"

I shook my head. "I tidied everything up the day before Sarah-Jane was born," I said. "I must have had a premonition."

- 12 -

One person I had come to know during my time at Blackwater & Green was Gerald Harper. He was the local manager of an insurance company and came to the Rye office regularly when he did his 'rounds' of business contacts once a fortnight or so. He was not the only representative to call regularly, but he was the one who was most knowledgable — and prepared to share that knowledge with a young solicitor who was still wet behind the ears so far as insurance was concerned. A good deal of instruction in the finer details of the various policies available, including their respective benefits and drawbacks, took place over lunch at a local hostelry. The lunch usually consisted of a sandwich and half a pint of bitter — until I became pregnant and changed my drink to ginger beer.

A tall man in his late thirties with a long nose, carefully brushed light brown hair, and handsome hazel eyes that were always filled with laughter, he never looked quite at home in a suit and tie. Although I never saw him when he wasn't working, I knew he enjoyed running, and I imagined he was much more comfortable in shorts and a running vest than hampered with business clothes. This was never more evident than when, much to my surprise, he appeared at my home with a huge bouquet of pink flowers on the sweltering summer solstice — the day after Sarah-Jane's birth.

Swathed in the soft folds of the white cotton lace nightdress that I had saved for the occasion and surrounded by flowers and cards, Sarah-Jane and I were holding court in

SOLICITING FROM HOME

the large bedroom under the eaves when my mother showed Gerry into the room. Simultaneously, my two visitors, Doctor Myles and our next door neighbour, Horace, had risen to their feet.

Myles had arrived with a beautiful box of chocolates, joking: "I give these to all my new mothers — it helps to keep them sweet." He'd grinned endearingly as he kissed my cheek and sat down. "Seriously, they may help tomorrow if you have an attack of the baby blues. Not that the blues are compulsory you understand."

With these words he lifted Sarah-Jane from her carry cot and was in the process of checking her over when Horace appeared with a joyously extravagant bunch of dahlias from his garden. Their yellow, red and orange petals sang of summer sunshine and the sight of them was immediately uplifting. Not that my spirits needed to be uplifted.

Horace pecked my cheek when I thanked him, before merely glancing at Sarah-Jane. His attention was immediately taken by my other visitor.

"Ah, Doctor! Just the person I wanted to see!" He glanced at me and away, embarrassed.

Myles seized the opportunity to say, with a smile that was only slightly forced: "I'm not on duty today, Horace."

"But I'm having a bit of difficulty...."

"I must away!" Myles declared just as Gerald appeared.

Horace pursued Myles down the stairs and I doubted he would get away without having to listen to Horace's problems. Poor Myles. That was the downside of having a country practice — you never got a day off. I grinned at the thought, remembering Mr and Mrs Brown insisting on executing their Wills that very morning. But that hadn't mattered a jot! I was so happy and pleased with myself for producing the perfect baby that a permanent smile had affixed itself to my lips.

Although I was revelling in all the attention, and particularly in the assiduous care of my dear mama, part of me felt guilty because I was not used to lying lazily in bed. But the other part of me knew that she was enjoying her self-imposed role as much as I was enjoying showing my firstborn off to my many visitors, so I had decided to simply relax and enjoy myself.

Gerry bent to inspect Sarah-Jane with an experienced eye — his wife having given birth to a daughter not three months previously — presented the bouquet to me and sat down on the chair next to the bed. My mother took the flowers away to arrange them and Gerry made himself comfortable, loosening his tie and undoing the top button of his shirt. His jacket was already draped round the back of the chair and his legs sprawled untidily when he sat down.

"How do you look so cool?" he said, mopping his brow with his handkerchief. "I swear it's the hottest day of the summer! And, by God, we've had a decent summer this year, haven't we? Almost too hot, some people say. Not that I'm one of them, I hasten to add."

"I don't feel very cool," I said, feeling my smile deepen, "but I'm lucky there's bit of a breeze up here. Mum opened all the windows, as you can see."

He sighed and leaned back in his chair. "Cool or not, you look blooming. No-one would guess that ..."

"You should have seen me earlier. No actually, you shouldn't. Let's just say, I look and feel a great deal better now. And haven't I been lucky? Just look at all this!" I threw

SOLICITING FROM HOME

out a hand to indicate all my lovely gifts, caught the glass of water mother had left on the bedside table, tried to catch it, failed and splashed the lot over his knees. "Oh dear! I'm so sorry. Let me…"

"Don't do anything, Melanie. That was exactly what I needed. The perfect way to cool off."

I felt myself blushing and started to apologise, but he held up his hand authoritatively. Instead, I said: "Thank you so much for such beautiful flowers."

"My pleasure. I'd been wanting to come and see how you were doing and you cleverly had the baby just before my day for visiting people in Rye. It gave me a wonderful excuse to drive across the Marsh with the car windows open. It's absolutely airless in the town."

Typical! I thought. He's driven nine miles to bring me a bouquet of flowers and we're talking about the weather. How very British!

"Actually, I had another reason for coming over this way. I have a couple of customers who need to have their insurance policies explained to them. I'd like to recommend you to them — but I thought I should at least have the courtesy to come and ask you first."

"How kind of you," I said, and meant it.

"Not that you'll be feeling like doing anything for a couple of weeks. There's no hurry. Take your time: see how you feel."

"No need for that, Gerry. I'd be delighted. I'm not doing much else at the moment." What a whopping lie, Melanie! I thought. You know you have no energy and that all you want to do is to sit and drool over your perfect baby all day and all night.

In the event, I was glad that Gerry knew more than I did about childbirth and its aftermath. After a euphoric couple of days, my spirits descended into the well-known after birth depression called the 'baby blues' and stayed there for the best part of a week. I suppose I'd been riding high on adrenaline but when the level of that hormone lessened, my spirits dropped like a stone. I could do nothing but cry. I was sore all over. Sarah-Jane was not feeding at all during the day but she was constantly hungry through the night. My nights were hot, sweaty and sleepless. My days were hot, sweaty and painful. On top of that, Sarah-Jane was losing weight. The round bonny baby was fast becoming a thin fretful one.

Ryan was useless. He worried — about me, about the baby, about lack of sleep, about work — about anyone and anything. My mother was there to help and reassure me, but she couldn't feed the baby. I felt helpless, completely lacking the skills or capability to deal with this demanding scrap of humanity. But there was nothing else for it: I simply had to learn to cope by myself.

When my father — who had been abroad when each of his own children were born and thus had had nothing to do with either my brother or myself until we were a few months old — arrived one day bearing a bottle of gripe water at arm's length, I finally realised that I had to stop feeling sorry for myself and concentrate on other things. From that moment on, probably thanks to the gripe water, Sarah-Jane began to take more milk and to sleep for correspondingly longer periods of time. Slowly I recovered my equanimity and realised that what I needed most was something to occupy my mind.

I had no sooner reached this conclusion than Gerald Harper appeared. He rolled up in an estate car that had seen better days both inside and out, bringing with him a couple of documents on which he needed my advice. I quickly put Sarah-Jane down for a sleep and expeditiously grabbed them from him. He declined my offer of coffee and made his escape, promising to return the next day.

By the following day, I had digested the documentation and was ready to give my suggestions. Gerry smiled as he pocketed my notes, promising that he would suggest his clients contacted me. Feeling disappointed in myself, I mentioned that I would need a little more time to learn how to cope with a baby before I could do anything more than make Wills. From then on, he made sure I was kept busy Will-writing.

I was back in the land of the truly living and back in business as well. As I began to blossom, so did Sarah-Jane. Ryan relaxed into the husband I had married, and we found ourselves happier than ever — if much more tired than before Sarah-Jane's birth. She was such an angelic baby. She slept soundly and often; smiled a lot; and, in fact, did everything early for her age.

When she was a week old, I took her to be inspected by Olive. After that, there was no doubt that I had found a treasure of a baby-minder who would look after Sarah-Jane whenever required. My mother, too, was keen to take on a granny role and came to help whenever she could. Although I couldn't bear to part with Sarah-Jane for more than an hour at a time, in-between feeds, that hour or two gave me time to start setting up my practice in earnest. I wrote to various organisations requesting agencies and accounts. A procession of representatives soon appeared on my doorstep.

Fanstory.com

A number of other representatives began calling at Rose Cottage. I felt so sorry for what had happened to young Mr Evans that I made sure I was better prepared when others came to call. I telephoned each of the organisations I had previously contacted and asked them to make sure they made a formal appointment before coming all the way to Oldchurch to see me.

Belatedly I had realised that it was because I had not made this clear that Mr Evans had suffered so much embarrassment. I had informed his firm that I was a solicitor who was setting up in practice. I should have known that they would ask a representative to call when next in the vicinity.

Added to that, I had given a High Street address. *I* knew it was my home, but that was not obvious unless one knew Oldchurch well. The poor young man had obviously expected to visit an office, probably to be seen by a secretary who would give him an order for stationery. I'm sure that the last thing he'd expected was to come into a home, greeted by someone who appeared to be the home help, and interviewed by a nursing mother.

I telephoned the Solicitors' Stationery Company to apologise, only to be told that Mr Evans was not available because he'd given in his notice. I was sad to hear this. I felt partly to blame for his sudden departure, but there was nothing more I could do, so I wished him well.

To this day, I wonder about him: I still hope that he was

SOLICITING FROM HOME

not too scarred by the incident and went on to bigger and better employment.

The next person to brave the Russell home was a representative of a local office furniture supplier. He called a few days after my mother had returned to her own home. By then, I had learned how to deal with Sarah-Jane's demands, mostly by feeding her whenever she wanted. I knew that I would have to insist on a routine eventually, but even my mother agreed that it was not vital.

When Percy Porter knocked on the door, Sarah-Jane was asleep in her basket in the nursery. Wishing I had had time to change into something more appropriate for a solicitor than tighter-than-they-should-be (blame Sarah-Jane) blue jeans and a yellow sweater with a brown ship's wheel embroidered on the front, I opened the front door to him with a flourish. He acknowledged my casual attire with an owlish blink.

Percy was shortish, tubbyish, fairish and of an indeterminate age somewhere between thirty and forty. His bluish eyes hidden behind the sort of spectacles that everyone wore. But he possessed a warmly genuine smile, which was unfortunately not in evidence when we first met.

"Um," he greeted me. "Urm ... Mrs Russell, I presume?" At my smile and nod he went on: "Percy Porter from Payne & Sons of Ashford. I think you're expecting me?"

"Of course," I said, "Do come in."

I led him into the dining room, this being the room that doubled as my interview room and so appeared a little more business-like than the rest of the house. Before long we were huddled together over numerous furniture catalogues.

After looking at desks and office machines for what seemed a very long time, I realised that Sarah-Jane would soon wake up and start yelling to be fed. I cut the conversation short.

"All I need at the moment is a large filing cabinet. Can you help me choose please?"

Mr Porter was obviously disappointed, but managed a brave smile, turning the page to reveal illustrations of grey filing cabinet after grey filing cabinet.

"They all look alike." I was vainly trying to see any difference between them other than the price.

"To be honest, they do. There's not a lot of difference," he said, looking me straight in the eye. "Mrs Russell, I'm going to be honest with you. I could sell you the top of the range of these cabinets and make a good commission. But you would soon find out that it was more than you needed and then you would not return to Payne & Sons as your office suppliers. So let me make you a promise — the same promise that I make to all my customers — I will never sell you a pup. I may well suggest you try something a little more expensive than the cheapest, but I promise you it will last. Can we shake hands on that?"

"With pleasure," I said, offering my hand.

Percy shook it, firmly. "I promise you will have no regrets about trusting me."

I had no idea how to react to his words so I changed the subject ever-so-slightly.

"Shall we go up to the bedroom now?"

Percy's face went white, then puce. Watching this amazing reaction to my simple question, I feared he was about to have a heart attack. Suddenly I understood. He

SOLICITING FROM HOME

thought I was propositioning him! He probably thought I was the other sort of woman who solicited from home. Oh dear! I felt my own cheeks flame before the funny side of the situation tickled my risible faculties, and I burst out laughing.

"I'm so sorry," I breathed when my laughter had subsided sufficiently to allow me to inhale. "I phrased that rather badly! It's just that I work from a desk in the bedroom, you see. I know where I would like to put the filing cabinet, but I'm not sure there's sufficient room. Would you come and measure?"

Without waiting for a reply, I led the way up the stairs. Percy followed, still looking bemused. His brow cleared when he saw the size of our bedroom and noted the desk in the corner, the filing trays and my typewriter.

"Oh, you really do work from here!"

The relief in his voice was so palpable that I was hard put to it to keep my laughter in check.

I tried to be businesslike. "Of course! Now this is where I work. I would like the filing cabinet — if possible one with four drawers — beside the desk, but I'm not sure if it will fit under the eaves. There's such a slope to the ceiling here, you see?"

"Yes, I see. Do you have a ruler?"

I supplied one from the desk.

"I think it will fit."

"That's wonderful!"

"A big one might be a trifle tight, so perhaps you'd prefer to try a smaller one?"

The double entendre too tempting to resist. My tongue ran away with itself without my mind's permission.

"As the bishop said ..." I stopped and felt myself blush to the roots of my hair.

Percy turned pink.

I felt my cheeks grow redder. Oh God! What must he think of me? Why couldn't I keep my mouth shut and my thoughts to myself? I was about to apologise when he started to chuckle.

"I'm a Christian, you know." *Oh No! I didn't.* "So I know a few bishops." *Melanie you idiot!* "And I know what they get up to! For that reason *my* version involves a French teacher and a gardener."

He winked at me.

With relief, I tried to make amends.

"Please forget I said that. Let's get back to office furniture. You think a three-drawer filing cabinet would be best? Then a three drawer one it shall be! I'll leave you to choose one for me."

He was still chuckling, but he said soberly: "Middle of the range, I suggest. Sufficiently substantial to last but not too heavy? Right. I promised you I would deal with you honestly, so this is the one I'd recommend."

He showed me the photograph in the catalogue.

"Great," I said, giving it a cursory glance. "When can you deliver it?"

He consulted his diary and gave me a date the following week. Then he winked again.

"And don't worry, I'll warn the delivery men that you'll invite them straight upstairs to your bedroom!"

I don't think the enormity of my behaviour struck me until he said that. I felt heat rise from the tips of my toes to my hairline. I raced downstairs ahead of him, sure I was as red as a beetroot.

That afternoon I was more than glad to see the back of Percy Porter, but over the years ahead he was to become a particular friend. He kept his word: he was always honest and he never 'sold me a pup'. He was a kind, good man on whom I could always rely.

I still smile when I remember that our business relationship began with an invitation to my bedroom!

The next gentleman to call was a different representative from the Solicitors Stationery Company. Older this time, thinner, only a little more at ease than his predecessor, and late for his appointment by nearly half an hour. He introduced himself as Wilson and proffered me a dead fish of a hand. I shook it firmly but it slithered away from mine, dropping, like his eyes, towards the carpet.

I offered him a seat at the dining table and a cup of coffee. He took a seat, but declined the coffee. He had scarcely been in the dining room more than five seconds before he told me that he had five children of whom he was very proud. I presumed that qualified him for the task of visiting me and made the mistake of asking: "And did your wife breastfeed them all?"

"Oh no, of course not! Bottled milk is so much better for them, you know."

Privately, I didn't know anything of the sort. How could it be better than what Nature provided? Breast milk was a commodity that cost nothing, was always available at the right temperature with no need for extra utensils and, since no sterilising was required, contained no horrid chemicals for the baby to imbibe. "Women's business anyway," he went on. "I keep well out of it."

I kept my opinion to myself and dissembled — as, in those days, all good young women should: I smiled a false smile and changed the subject.

"I have a list here of the forms I need, which are mostly to do with conveyancing. I need different kinds of engrossment paper, too."

He sighed, and took out a long form with a great deal of small print on its reverse. Barking out questions, he proceeded to fill in the form with my answers, or at least his version of them. He was surprised that I could remember my bank account number without having to check, but wrote it down anyway. However, he couldn't resist asking for a copy of the bank statement to check the number. I found the opening statement which showed nothing more than a deposit of one hundred pounds. I informed him it was the best I could do since I would not receive one showing any activity until a couple of weeks hence; and in return he told me that his company would need a banker's reference before the account could be opened.

"Of course," I concurred. He had been late for his appointment and all the paperwork had taken longer than I had expected. Now a tightness was spreading across my bosom. I knew that any moment Sarah-Jane would wake up and once she started crying she would not stop until I fed her. This man obviously disapproved of such natural functions — I could not feed Sarah-Jane in front of him. I had to get him out of my house fast.

Unfortunately he was settling in for the duration. "Let me advise you about those forms you say you need."

"No, please don't worry! I've already checked with ..."

"They may be out-of-date," he interrupted. "They're

always bringing out new ones."

He picked up the list just as Sarah-Jane let out a piercing cry. He jumped.

"What was that?"

"My baby's just woken up. I'll have to feed her soon."

"Let me check this..."

"It's quite all right. Why don't you take the list with you? You can telephone me when the account's approved and then ..."

"It would be much better to do it now, so that I can explain it all to you."

I felt like braining him. Or yelling at him that I was quite capable of understanding conveyancing forms. I couldn't see what he would need to explain about supplying me with the correct paper for engrossing Wills.

"I'd prefer to do it over the phone," I said, standing up just as Sarah-Jane's cries changed pitch. She was furious. The man flinched, but his tone did not alter.

"My instructions are to explain all the company's requirements and to make sure that you understand ..."

"I understand. But I have to feed my baby now." He was still sitting, still looking up at me, as I left the room and he was in the exactly the same position when I returned with a screaming baby.

"Mrs Russell," he began.

"I have to feed my baby *now*," I told him, sitting down at the table with the bawling infant in my arms.

He looked exasperated. "Can't you put it somewhere else?" he said. "This can't be hurried."

And at that moment my nipples responded to Sarah-Jane's cries with twin jets of milk. As I felt the liquid soak the front of my blouse, I saw his eyes drawn to that part of my anatomy. Squirming with embarrassment inside, I drew myself up haughtily and began to unbutton myself.

"Mr Wilson," I said, raising my voice above Sarah-Jane's wails. "I have to feed my baby. I would prefer not to do it in front of you, but you give me no option."

Halfway through this speech, Mr Wilson thrust his chair from the table, stood up and almost ran to the door.

"I'll telephone. Goodbye."

And with that he was gone. He never returned. Nor did he telephone. My account was set up with no problems and all transactions were done by post or over the telephone with a charming older woman in the ordering department.

The first time she heard my name I heard her trying to smother her laughter.

"Ah, you're the lady who terrified Mr Wilson, aren't you? What did you do to him?" My explanation caused more laughter. "You may like to know that he hasn't fully recovered yet. He is far more polite to us all in the office than he used to be."

I reckoned that was another way of saying that he was less of a prig and a little more human. Maybe Sarah-Jane and I had taught him something that he had not learned from his own five children, or maybe he just had not known how to deal with a woman in what he considered to be a man's role. But it was most likely that I had embarrassed him as much as his presence had unsettled me.

Yet another young man came to see me the following year, but by then Sarah-Jane was with her baby minder and I was happily installed in a proper office of my own.

On the morning Mr Terence Tate telephoned me, I was

SOLICITING FROM HOME

expecting a Building Society Manager to knock on the door within five minutes.

For once, I was ready: I had put Sarah-Jane down to sleep, brushed my unruly hair, checked that my eye-liner had not run and re-applied my lipstick. I'd also made sure that the dining room was clean and tidy, the kettle was boiling, cups ready and that there was sufficient milk in the fridge. Finally, I'd dashed back upstairs to change my bespattered top for a simple pink teeshirt. It seemed tighter than I remembered, especially around the bust, but there was nothing else in my cupboard that was clean and ironed, so it had to do.

When the phone rang I was on my way downstairs, so by the time I snatched up the receiver I was breathless.

"Hello," I gasped. "Mrs Russell speaking."

A pause on the other end of the line. Then:

"Is that Mrs Russell, the solicitor?" asked a light voice with a slight Yorkshire accent.

"Yes," I said, thinking this might be a new client. "Can I help you?"

"I'm sure you can, Mrs Russell. I received a letter from you last week."

I felt the crease between my brows. I'd written to a number of people the previous week to arrange all the necessary contacts and accounts to help me get my practice off the ground.

"I don't think you told me your name?"

"I'm sorry. My name is Terrence Tate. I'm the manager of Folkestone Building Society."

"Oh!" I hoped I didn't sound disappointed. But why on earth was he telephoning me now? "Mr Tate ... of course, how nice ... I'm expecting you."

"I know. I do apologise. I'm afraid I've been held up. I'm phoning to tell you I've been delayed...." Oh No! Surely this wasn't going to go the same way as Mr Wilson's visit? I had such a small window of opportunity for serious discussions between Sarah-Jane's feeds. "...But I shouldn't be more than ten minutes late at the outside."

Thank God for that!

"That's fine. I'll be waiting."

I doubt it was more than five minutes before the door knocker banged. When I opened the front door, a tall, thin man, probably in his mid-thirties, was standing on the doorstep. I noticed he was wearing a rather horrible brown suit, white shirt and knitted tie and that, from above a long aquiline nose, hooded grey eyes were regarding me with an expression of amusement.

I smiled in response and a sudden beam lit up his narrow face. I noticed he looked me up and down before he took a step back. For a few moments we stared at each other in mutual scrutiny.

"Mrs Russell?"

"Mr Tate?"

We both laughed and I moved aside, indicating that he should enter. His eyes danced and his mouth twitched.

"Would you like a cup of coffee?"

"Very much."

By the time I carried two mugs of coffee — one black (I was slimming) and one white with two sugars (it was so annoying that thin people never seemed to have to watch their calorie intake) — into the dining room, he had obviously already made up his mind about me. All the

SOLICITING FROM HOME

necessary forms that would enable me to apply to be a Building Society agent were spread across the table.

"You just need to sign here ... and here," he directed. "I've heard about you from Mr Piper at Blackwater & Green."

"Oh?"

"Yes, I went to see him about a problem with one of his clients. When we'd dealt with that, he mentioned that you might be applying to be an agent of the Society. He endorsed you in glowing terms."

"Oh!" I felt my cheeks crimson.

He promptly changed the subject.

"I'll need a copy of your Law Society practising certificate, please."

I was prepared for this and had obtained a certified photocopy in readiness: I passed it to him. He gathered it up with all the other documentation and stowed it away in his battered briefcase, but showed no sign of moving. He leant back in his chair and sipped his coffee.

We slipped easily into conversation. I learned all about his family: he was married with three children who were all at grammar school. And he asked about mine, and why I had decided to set up my own legal practice. This was my cue: I couldn't resist relaying the anecdote about how I had visited my bank manager, Mr Standish, to ask for a loan, and how he had not only granted it, but had insisted that Oldchurch needed a solicitor and gone were my hopes of being a stay-at-home mum.

Terrence chuckled. "I hope you will be my guest at the next Business Club meeting in Folkestone. You would bring a breath of fresh air to a rather stuffy affair!"

I must have looked as astonished as I felt because he went on: "I know it's a long way to come, but you would meet a lot of local business people. As you probably know, around here it's not *what* you know, but *who* you know that counts. I can introduce you to other Building Society managers, estate agents, bank managers, but ..." His voice trailed off.

"What aren't you telling me?" I teased, smiling.

The answering smile vanished from his face. "I'm afraid you would be the only woman there. Would you mind?"

"Not at all. I'm used to it. Thank you for the invitation."

We chatted for a few more minutes; but as soon as Sarah-Jane awoke with a wail, Terrence Tate stood up.

"I think it's time for me to leave. May I say what a pleasure it's been to meet you?"

"You may, indeed! It's been a pleasure for me, too."

"I'm sure we'll meet again soon. I'll be in touch."

Like dear Mr Standish, Terrence Tate proved to be another good angel. He introduced me to many local agents and businessmen and generally smoothed my business path. Without him, my practice would have grown much more slowly than it did. It was only in later years that I understood how much he had helped me.

Without him and Mr Standish, my practice would probably have been dead in the water because most business on the Marsh was transacted between contacts met through the Rotary or Lions Clubs or at Freemasons' meetings. As a woman, all those societies were closed to me: I could only pick up their leavings like any scavenger. Mind you, I did pick up some of those leavings, especially when I felt people had been discriminated against. Some of those matters were

SOLICITING FROM HOME

very lucrative, others were not, but — like Mrs Kendall's — they brought me a great deal of job satisfaction as well as ongoing work.

Terrence Tate and I became good friends, meeting for a business lunch about once a month. These were enjoyable occasions in their own right, but there was a great deal more to them than that, for Terrence and I discussed many interesting matters over a meal, and because he trusted my opinion, I am sure that he approved several mortgages that might not otherwise have been accepted by the Building Society. I am pleased to say that none of the clients I referred to him ever let me — or him — down.

It was perhaps six months after our first meeting that he confided in me the reason for his telephone call.

"I arrived early in Oldchurch," he said. "I drove up and down the High Street and eventually located your house. But it didn't look at all like an office. The more I thought about it, the more worried I became. I began to get cold feet. I wondered if you would prove to be some eccentric old bag. I knew Mr Piper had given you an excellent reference. The questions I asked myself were: 'Why? Was it because he was keen to be rid of you?' The more I thought about it the worse it got! So when I saw a telephone box I decided I would ring and make my excuses."

"But you didn't. Why not?"

"When I heard your voice, I liked you instantly. I realised I was being stupid."

"So that was why you arrived so promptly!"

"And when I did ... shall we just say that you were quite different from what I was expecting?"

"Different? How?"

Melanie Russell

"You were as attractive as your voice! And I'd never before seen a lady solicitor wearing jeans and a skinny tee shirt!"

I blushed, but I was flattered, nonetheless.

- 13 -

There followed an interesting time as I gradually equipped myself with the tools I required. The old portable typewriter outlasted my expectations. Many a Will did I type on that ancient machine, but eventually the sticky 's' broke off entirely when I was typing an engrossment and it had to go.

In a panic, I telephoned my old boss, Mr Chamberlain of Blackwater & Green.

"Hello, Melanie. To what do I owe this pleasure?" he greeted me.

"A disaster, I'm afraid. My old typewriter has finally given up the ghost and I have a Will to engross by tomorrow morning. I wondered if …"

"Of course, Melanie. Bring it in. I'll ask Sandra to type it for you."

"Actually, would it be all right with you if I typed it myself?"

"Oh, I'm not sure if we can have a solicitor doing her own typing."

"It would be much easier. You see, I don't have a dictaphone."

"Well, if you're sure. We'll see you later."

When I reached the office a couple of hours later, Mr Chamberlain's personal secretary, Sandra, conducted me to the room where the post was usually opened and there on the table sat a typewriter, Will paper, a typing rubber, needle, scissors, black tape and various other items she thought I might need.

"Have I remembered everything? Or is there something else you need?" she asked anxiously.

"I can't think of *anything*, Sandra."

When I thanked her profusely, she looked gratified, but she only smiled and said: "I know — a cup of coffee! I'll get one for you now."

The cup of coffee was long gone and I was typing the execution clause on the last page of the engrossment when Mr Chamberlain came in.

"I'm sorry I wasn't here when you arrived, Melanie. I hope you have all you need?"

"I can't tell you how grateful…" I began but he waved my thanks aside.

"I've been talking to Jeremy and we have a proposition for you."

He smiled. and I felt my eyebrows rise enquiringly although I said nothing.

"As you know, we're in the process of updating some of our equipment. We wondered whether you would be interested in taking some of the old stuff off our hands? We have a couple of manual typewriters that still have some life in them — the girls far prefer electric ones now, you know. They are a lot faster and the fingering is lighter. We have some old recording equipment as well which you might find a home for?"

"Thank you," I breathed, "That would be wonderful. Er… how much would you want…"

"No charge, Melanie. You'll be doing us a favour. We both think of you as our protégée, and want to help where we can. Just come back and see us sometimes. Let us know

SOLICITING FROM HOME

how you're doing."

And so I took the typewriter home with me along with two boxes full of other equipment. By the time I was ready to drive home, I was teary-eyed with gratitude. I was to find that this was only the first of many kindnesses extended to me over the next few months, from people in all walks of life.

Because I was working from home, resulting in all sorts of inconveniences for my clients, I initially made no charge for my services. Although it literally meant I was working for nothing, I thought that it would at least provide some form of publicity, since, as I have said, the Solicitors' Practice Rules banned me from advertising. I was right in this for the word travelled fast all round Oldchurch: I soon found I had to turn people away simply because I had neither time nor facilities.

The amazing thing was that I did not lack for payment. Gifts appeared right, left and centre. The butcher sent round a different joint of meat each week for three months; the baker sent a collection of cakes and refused payment for the bread I 'bought' at his shop; and a dear old gentleman sent me a dozen bottles of gin that must have been sitting in his cellar for years as the price tags were in 'old' money — the pounds, shillings and pence which was the currency before decimalisation in February 1971.

The fishmonger rang the doorbell one morning and thrust a box into my hands, a box containing fish so fresh that a couple of them promptly flipped themselves on to the floor, much to Poppadum's fascinated disgust. I must admit that the fish were not my favourite form of barter.

I also received pots of jam, chutney and honey, fresh

vegetables, soft toys for Sarah-Jane, a knitted hat and scarf for me — and a prong-hoe.

Ryan was absolutely delighted with the hoe, soon putting it to use heaping up the earth round the potatoes — seed potatoes had been another 'gift'. Coming in from the garden, sweaty, dirty and smiling, he grabbed me to him, and kissed me thoroughly.

"You may not be making any money, Mel, but we certainly eat well!"

There were sadnesses as well as joys, of course.

The first Wills I made were for people who were terminally ill. While Mr White survived happily for some years, Jennifer died just after her Will was completed.

I'm pleased to say that the more Wills I prepared, more people survived than died after availing themselves of my services. But for those who died soon after a Will was drawn, I could comfort myself with the knowledge that I had helped the deceased to ensure that his or her last wishes were respected. It was also good to be able to help the surviving spouses, or other executors, to deal with all the paperwork and legal requirements that followed a death.

Gerald Harper came to see me one day and asked if I would act for a young man and his wife who were considering taking out a life policy and a mortgage protection policy. They needed independent advice and I had no hesitation in agreeing.

Within a few days Mr and Mrs Black were sitting in my dining room, papers spread before them on the table as I explained the relative merits and disadvantages of several different policies. The differences were significant but

SOLICITING FROM HOME

unfortunately, as is often the case, no particular policy stood out as having the best terms.

Mr Black was a shy man in his early thirties, plump and balding, with a sudden smile. His wife was a petite blonde with a wasp-like waist and a waspish manner. She looked so young it was almost impossible to believe that they had three children aged between eleven and four years.

By the time I had completed my explanation of the policies they were both looking bemused.

"Let's run through the main points," I suggested. They each nodded, he eagerly, she with an odd diagonal tilt to her head.

"First of all, may I say 'well done' for considering taking out life insurance cover? So many people don't — which is not a problem as long as they stay fit, well and employed."

I paused to give time for my words to sink in.

"But you have given it thought — which is more than sensible since you have young children. It's really important that you are covered financially in case one — or both — of you dies..."

Valerie Black shuddered. "Someone just walked over my grave."

I shivered, but tried to mask it. I didn't want to give any credence to the thought so I went on: "Some of these policies also cover you against personal injury ..."

"We're hardly likely to need that, are we? We're not exactly taking risks."

I let Valerie's remark pass. I would explain later. At the moment I needed to keep on track. "... or provide cover in case you become so ill or disabled that you can no longer work."

Valerie raised one eyebrow. "That's very unlikely!" she said.

"You recently bought your own house, didn't you?" I checked.

"Yes, there's still a lot of work to be done on it," said Donald Black. "But it's all ours."

"The children can't believe it!" Valerie enthused. "They have a bedroom each, now. It's been a bit of a stretch financially but we've finally made it."

She squeezed her husband's hand and he picked up hers and kissed it. They smiled at each other affectionately; and I thought how lucky the children were to have parents who were still so much in love with each other. I didn't want to have to make them think of difficulties and disasters, but that was my job.

"And I'm sure you'd hate to lose it now that it's yours. But have you thought what would happen if you died, Mr Black?"

"That's why we're here," he said. "I *keep* thinking of it — especially since we made our Wills. The solicitor who acted for us on the purchase of our house insisted on that. There's nothing like making a Will to make you realise you're mortal."

"No," I agreed soberly.

"I drive to North Kent every day. It makes me wonder: what if I were killed in a road accident? How would Valerie manage?"

"Don't be silly, Don. You're not going to die. Neither am I."

"But, darling... It could happen."

"Nonsense," Valerie rejoined. "I won't have you thinking

SOLICITING FROM HOME

that way."

"Okay, tell me how would you manage?" he demanded.

"I'd manage. I'd have to."

"But you don't work. You haven't worked since Marie was born eleven years ago. What about the house? How could you pay the mortgage?"

"Oh! you're being too depressing. If it ever comes to that, we'll see. But it's not going to. I won't have it."

"It's as well to have some insurance..." I began. But Valerie rounded on me.

"And what do *you* get out of this, I'd like to know?"

"Actually, I don't."

"Pull the other one!" Valerie's sudden anger was barely held in check. "There's got to be something! Don't tell me you're doing this out of the goodness of your heart?"

"Actually ..."

"I'm not listening to any more. Come on Don, we're going."

"Valerie, I really think you ought to give Mrs Russell a chance to speak."

"Speak? Chance? She's been doing nothing but speak all this time. And what have we heard? It doesn't matter which policy we take out. As long as we choose one. And as long as she gets her commission."

With that she stood up so forcefully that her chair crashed to the floor. She ignored it and flounced towards the door

"Well? Are you coming?"

Don Black stood up with a deep sigh. He shrugged. "I'm sorry, Mrs Russell. You see how it is."

I'd been thoroughly surprised by the turn of events and

had kept uncharacteristically quiet. Completely unused to having my motives questioned, let alone wilfully misunderstood, I was indulging in a fit of pique mixed with self-pity. How could she think that of me? I had nothing to gain, whether they initiated a policy or not. I would earn no commission ... and yes! I *was* doing this from the goodness of my heart. I decided that, far from admiring their relationship, Mr Black was welcome to her! Now I pitied their poor children, thinking they would never be allowed to express any opinion other than their mother's.

The papers were still strewn across the table. I collected them together, keeping my head down to hide my expression. When I had my temper under control I spoke quietly.

"Yes, I see. But I urge you to think carefully. I do recommend that you take out at least one of these policies."

I handed the collection to him. And now I was able to attempt to make my peace with his wife, I looked at her.

"I'm sorry you think that I'm in this for my own advantage. That is not the case."

Valerie shrugged but had the grace to look uncomfortable.

I could not resist urging: "Please think about it, at least. If only for the sake of your children."

"Don't you dare talk to me in that patronising tone! I *always* think of *my* children. But this has nothing to do with them."

She slammed out of the front door without even saying goodbye.

"I apologise for my wife," Don whispered to me, looking over my shoulder in the direction Valerie had gone. "We *will* think about it and I'll talk her round." I smiled and he smiled back. "It'll just take a little time. She doesn't like to think of death and illness. I appreciate your help and understanding. Thank you."

He shook my hand and left more quietly than his spouse. I sat without moving, waiting for my anger to subside.

A few minutes later I heard Ryan's key in the lock. My delight in seeing him dismissed any residual bad feeling I was harbouring towards Mr and Mrs Black.

But for three consecutive nights afterwards I woke in the early morning worrying that none of the policies had been acceptable to them. Much to my relief, after the third night, Mr Black telephoned to make an appointment. I could hear the smile in his voice as he told me that he had convinced his wife that they should both take out life policies.

"I'm very glad to hear that," I said. "Have you decided which ones you prefer?"

"Definitely Mr. Harper's company."

"That's good. When would you like to come?"

"Would this evening be convenient?"

No, not convenient exactly, I thought, but I could rearrange my evening.

"Yes, about what time?"

"I'll be there as soon as possible after work," Don Black promised. "I usually get home at about six thirty. Are you sure that's not too late?"

"That will be fine, I'll look forward to seeing you then." I said, thinking that I would prepare a meal for Ryan and myself in readiness and we would eat after they had gone.

I was so pleased that I did a little dance. Everything was

working out after all. I knew they couldn't be in better hands than Gerry's. All the Blacks would have to do was sign the appropriate proposal form. I would do my bit and Gerry would do the rest. And Ryan would be around to look after Sarah-Jane, and to witness their signatures should a second witness be required. Perfect!

When Ryan came home, I warned him the Blacks were coming for a consultation, showed him the cold meat, baked potatoes and simple salad I'd prepared, and told him to eat without me if I was delayed.

Then I closed myself in the dining room and waited. Half past six came and went.

"Darl, I'm famished! Can we eat now?" Ryan yelled from the sitting room.

Thinking that Don Black must have been delayed by traffic, I put Ryan's supper on a tray and started feeding Sarah-Jane, ready to pass her to her father should the Blacks arrive. Sarah-Jane took her fill and Ryan's plate emptied fast.

But no one came. No-one telephoned. I checked the clock again and again. By the time half past seven arrived with no message my concern was fast becoming apprehension.

At seven forty-five I telephoned Valerie Black. The phone rang and rang, but no-one picked up the receiver. I thought about eating, but I was no longer hungry.

At eight o'clock I put all the remaining food away in the refrigerator. I telephoned again. Still no reply. I put Sarah-Jane to bed and tidied the dining room. Ryan was flicking though the television channels and invited me to join him on the sofa, but I couldn't settle.

I opted for a good long soak in the bath with a book to distract me. From what I needed to be distracted I did not

SOLICITING FROM HOME

know, because it was most likely that the Blacks had forgotten their appointment. If they'd forgotten, they would not have thought to telephone me. I refused to put a name to my worries, hoping that it was simply a case of misunderstanding. But I had an uncomfortable feeling of precognition.

Eventually, I went to bed. Ryan followed soon after. Not wanting to talk about the possibilities, I feigned sleep until I heard his gentle snores, but, try as I might, I could not go to sleep myself. In the morning I dragged myself out of bed feeling that I had not slept a wink.

The following morning I tried again to telephone Valerie, but was unable to get through because the line was constantly engaged. After my fourth abortive attempt to speak to her, I telephoned the operator and asked for the line to be checked, hoping that someone had simply forgotten to replace the receiver and left the line open.

The operator reported back to me that the line was open and that voices were speaking on it. I dialled again, to no avail. The line was still busy. I tried to settle to other things, but found myself pacing with anxiety. My anxiety unsettled Sarah-Jane and she was unusually fractious.

'This is ridiculous!' I admonished myself. 'It's not as though they're anything to do with you, really. Just calm down. All will be well.'

But all was not well. At half past twelve Gerald telephoned

"Have you heard?"

"Heard what?"

"About the accident."

"No." My heart skipped a beat and I fell into a chair.

"Tell me."

"It happened last night."

"Not Mr Black?" I interrupted. "Please tell me it's not Mr. Black!"

There was a pause at the other end of the line. "I'm sorry Melanie, I thought you would know."

"Know? How could I know? How do *you* know, anyway?"

"His wife telephoned. She wanted to know if he was covered."

"Oh no!" I noticed, in a distracted sort of way, that my fingers clutching the receiver were white with small pink patches. "Oh no!"

"It was all over the news last night. Didn't you hear?"

"No," I whispered, but I'd known something was wrong, hadn't I? "No," I said, more strongly. "I didn't see the news or listen to the radio."

"Mr Black was driving home along the motorway, apparently in a hurry. He was overtaking a lorry when it pulled out unexpectedly, crashed into his car and pushed it over the central reservation directly into the path of an oncoming vehicle. There was a seven car pile-up."

"How is he?"

The silence at the other end told its own story.

"He's dead, isn't he?"

"Yes. Killed instantly."

Stupidly, I found myself unable to speak.

"Are you all right, Melanie?" Gerry's voice was concerned.

"I'm sorry, Gerry. I'm quite all right. It was just such a shock."

SOLICITING FROM HOME

"I know. I'm sorry I was so blunt."

"No, it's me. I had a premonition, that's all."

"Premonition?"

"I know. Sounds stupid. He and his wife were supposed to come and see me last night to sign the proposal forms. I was worried when they didn't turn up but I thought they must have forgotten. Especially when there was no reply when I phoned."

"So they didn't sign?"

"I don't think so. Mr Black said he wanted to do it in front of me to make sure he got it right."

He sighed. "It's horrible to say this, but in a way, I'm glad."

"Why? What do you mean?"

"Even if he'd signed the papers last night, the company wouldn't have received them or the premium. That means the proposal wouldn't have been accepted and he wouldn't have been covered anyway."

"Yes," I said slowly. "I see that. But why are you glad?"

"For you," he said. "You might have been in a difficult position if he'd signed the papers and given you a cheque for the premium — and you hadn't submitted them to the company before his death. It's just possible his wife might have taken out a negligence claim against you."

"Thank you for thinking of me."

We said our goodbyes and Gerald promised to call round later in the week.

Gerald was very kind, but he'd mistaken the cause of my unhappiness. I knew that he had intended to give me a crumb of comfort, but his words hadn't touched the emptiness I was feeling.

I was troubled that Valerie had taken offence at something I'd said. That was why she'd stormed out. If only I'd phrased my words better! I knew it was no good explaining my feelings to either Gerald or Ryan. They would both say that I had done my best, that it was the Blacks' own decision not to sign when they first came for an appointment, and that I should not worry about it.

I went upstairs feeling distress, annoyance and self-blame. I found it hard to forgive myself for not insisting that they at least submitted a proposal for a life policy when they were with me. The policy would have been in force by now.

A few days later Valerie Black phoned to invite me to Don's funeral. She wasn't sure when it would be taking place because the police had said his body would not be released until after the autopsy had been completed.

"I'd like you to come. I know you were trying to help us both."

"Thank you. I'll be there." I couldn't think what else to say, but it didn't matter because she was still speaking.

"Mr Harper said you were blaming yourself because we had no insurance. It wasn't your fault. I shouldn't have been so hasty. It was only..." Her voice caught. "I couldn't bear the thought of him dying. I didn't want to think about it. But I'm going to have a long time to think about it now."

I felt my heart go out to her. Her voice failing, she quickly said goodbye and put the receiver down, but her words had set me thinking.

The funeral took place a fortnight later. The beautiful church of All Saints, the Cathedral of the Marshes, was packed. People from all parts of the community had come

SOLICITING FROM HOME

together to support the young widow and her three little daughters.

I knew that support would not stop when the funeral ended. Valerie would find people bringing gifts, offers of help would abound, and her daughters would be given treats and taken on outings. Not for them the silent, closed-up grief of the city-dwelling bereaved. They would be given time and space, but they would be the recipients of all sorts of kindnesses from friend and stranger alike.

My gift was the offer of help with obtaining Probate of Don's Will and with winding up his Estate. Valerie gratefully accepted, although I was sure she had no idea of the amount of work, nor of the distress she would be saved.

I had an ulterior motive as well. I believed that Don's Estate would be able to make a claim for damages against the driver of the lorry that hit his car. No matter that he, too, was dead. The claim would be against the employers of the lorry driver who ought to be insured against the negligence of their employee. I knew that, although it would take a long time to resolve, the compensation Valerie would receive would be substantial. In fact, it might well be a great deal more than the proceeds of a life policy.

So it proved, eventually. It took more than three years to obtain a settlement from the employer's insurers, but the amount Valerie received made it well worth the wait.

Although she did not marry again she gradually recovered her equilibrium. She had been a qualified hairdresser before she married and so she used some of the compensation to start her own hairdressing business. The salon proved very successful, and provided her with much-needed company and gossip. Soon she was serving coffee to her customers while they were waiting; and before long she expanded the business into the next-door shop by opening the first coffee bar in the town.

And so, as she coped with the sadness of Don's death, a new door opened — not only for Valerie and her girls, but also for the whole of Oldchurch.

- 14 -

A day or so later, I was enjoying the luxury of my new executive chair. Percy Porter had arrived with it half an hour earlier, assembling it while I made him a mug of coffee. He watched with amusement as I spun round on it a couple of times, grinning when I leaned back and put my feet up on the dining table, crossing my ankles as I'd seen American journalists do in films.

"Very clever, Mrs. Russell, but perhaps not entirely ladylike?"

I swept my feet back to the floor and sat up primly, straightening my back as well as my face. "Quite, Mr Porter. Is this better?"

At that moment I heard a knock on the front door. Both Percy and I started. Poppadum barked. I fixed her with a glare and she lay down, but not without a groan of protest. "I think that was the front door," I said, rising hurriedly to my feet. "Not that I'm expecting anyone."

"I must be going," Percy declared, heading for the kitchen with his empty mug. "Keep the chair on approval for the next fortnight. You can tell me if you want to keep it when I next call. Thanks for the coffee."

I shut Poppadum in the sitting room, much to her chagrin. I made for the front door, but before I reached it someone knocked again, hesitantly. As I'd surmised from the sound, the woman who stood on the doorstep looked distinctly nervous.

"Good afternoon. I think ... I'm not sure ... Mr Standish said ... I am looking for Mrs Russell, the solicitor. Are you she?"

"Good afternoon. Yes, I'm Melanie Russell," I said quickly, since she seemed on the verge of running away. I invited her to come in and she did so, hesitating in the tiny lobby between the two rooms. Percy reappeared from the kitchen and startled her so much she trembled, eyes looking from one to the other of us and back again.

"I didn't realise ... I'm sorry. I didn't mean to interrupt."

"No, it's fine. Mr Porter is just leaving."

I bade him a quick goodbye and requested the woman to follow me into the dining room. I motioned her to a chair.

"Do sit down."

"Beatrice Basset," she introduced herself, icy fingertips glancing against mine as she bobbed down quickly. I sat too, feeling very proud of my new executive chair.

"What can I do for you?"

Of medium height, plump, with a pink complexion, pale blue eyes and mouse-brown hair, my latest client perched on the edge of her chair, clasping her handbag in both hands.

"I want an injunction!" she quavered. "I don't care what it costs — well, I do, actually — but I just can't take any more. They're driving me mad. Quite literally. Mad."

She had clearly screwed up all her courage to come and see me. Her glittering eyes had been fixed on me, but now they slid away.

"I'll need to take a few details before I can advise you," I said, wondering whether every client that Mr Standish sent to me would be hanging onto their sanity by a thread.

SOLICITING FROM HOME

"Of course," she whispered, her eyes cast down towards her handbag.

"However," I continued, smiling in an attempt to take the sting from what I had to say. "I should tell you that injunctions can be difficult to obtain. Although the Court may grant what's called an Interim Injunction immediately — provided we have sufficient evidence of harm or real fear — it may only last fourteen days. To make it permanent we will have to have very strong evidence."

"What details do you need?" she asked breathlessly.

"Your name, address and phone number to start with."

She supplied the information in a voice just a touch above a whisper.

"Thank you," I said when I'd finished scribbling down her particulars. "Let's start at the beginning. Who are 'they'?"

"I don't know exactly," she almost-whispered. "If I did, I'd have given them a piece of my mind before now. There are youngsters who plague me but I think this is something much more sinister."

"Okay," I suggested, considering the matter. "Let's put that to one side for a moment. What are the youngsters doing to distress you so much?"

"They bang on my window. And look in making horrible faces. They swear too."

"Do you know any of these youngsters by name?" I asked. "Could you give me their names and addresses?"

Miss Basset's small nose twitched and she looked apprehensive.

"I know one or two of them. It's frightening when you're

on your own."

"I know. I'm sorry to press you, but can you give me their names?" If not, I thought wearily, this will go nowhere.

Reluctantly, she said: "Jimmy Gibbs and Matthew Denton."

"How old are they?" I asked.

"About twelve," she replied.

I laid my pencil down. "I'm afraid you can't take out an injunction against a minor. I suggest I have a word with our local policeman, Martin. He'll give them a warning and that should be the end of it," I said, thinking that calling on Martin to sort things out was becoming a habit.

She looked at me, alarm mixed with resignation. "*No!* No. I've asked him already. He spoke to them. They've stopped doing it since. It's other things now." She leaned forward confidingly. "I hear things. It sounds as though there's something — or someone — under my cottage."

"What sort of sounds? Things?" I demanded.

"You'll think I'm mad."

"No," I reassured her. "I'm very serious. Something or someone has obviously frightened you very badly. I want to find out what it is. And then I want to see if there's anything I can do to help you."

"Do you?" she questioned, apparently amazed. "You believe me? And you want to help? Oh, thank you."

She started to cry. Fishing a handkerchief from her sleeve, she blew her nose. I gave her a minute or two to compose herself and then I said gently: "That's right. But I can't help you unless you tell me everything."

Beatrice took a deep breath and sniffed loudly, her

SOLICITING FROM HOME

nostrils pinching together.

"I live alone now. My mother died last year and I nursed her to the end. I am lonely and it's very quiet round by the churchyard. There's hardly any traffic, you see. But recently…"

"How recently?" I interrupted.

She considered. "I suppose it started about three months ago. There was a lot of larking about in the churchyard by those boys — the ones I mentioned and their cronies. It had been so quiet until then."

"What did they do?"

"In the beginning they just rode around on their bikes, laughing and generally mucking about. It was a nuisance but boys will be boys! Then one day I found them smoking. I told them they were too young and that I would tell their parents if I saw them doing it again."

"And did you?"

"No, they seemed abashed. But the next day they were there again, smoking — and this time they had a bottle of beer. Actually it was probably more than one bottle. I was walking towards them, quite purposefully I expect, and the next thing I knew a beer bottle flew past my head — so close that I could feel it. Well! That was the last straw."

"Quite," I said, with feeling. "What happened next?"

"I marched up to them and told them I was going to report them to the police. That bottle could have killed me!"

"Did you see who actually threw the bottle?"

"No. But I'm sure it was one of them."

"You're certain?" I pressed. "It was definitely either Jimmy Gibbs or Matthew Denton?"

"N...no," she quavered. "I can't say it was *definitely* either of them. But I am sure the bottle was thrown from that direction by someone among their crowd."

"I see. And then?"

"After that they started to bang on my window. I'd find dogs' excrement on my doorstep and one day the tyres on my bicycle were slashed. I didn't have a moment's rest. Even when it was quiet I was waiting for it to start again."

"And it's still happening?"

"Yes. No." She clasped her hands together and bit her thin lower lip. "After Martin spoke to the youngsters they stopped terrorising me. But the other noises started."

"I'll come to that. But, first, tell me ... did they do the same things to anyone else?"

"No, that's the odd thing. They wait until I'm alone, when the neighbours are out or have their televisions on loudly — they're all deaf, my neighbours. I know one of my neighbours had a word with them and I expected them to start on her. But no, they're as sweet as pie to her."

"Correct me if I'm wrong, but it seems that you haven't actually seen anyone do any of those things recently? Even those you *think* Jimmy and Matthew are doing? Am I right?" I asked, softening my words by adding: "If I'm to help you, I need to know what real evidence there is, you see."

Beatrice considered for a moment and then said, with a firmness in her voice that had been absent before: "Yes, you are right. I haven't *seen* Jimmy or Matthew or anyone else do anything except make faces at me through the window. But truly, Mrs Russell, it is very, *very* frightening. When I hear the noises they're so loud, *and* so close, that I'm convinced I have intruders in the house."

"Does this happen at any particular time?"

"No, but it's nearly always after dark. Sometimes it's three in the morning."

"And you've spoken to Martin?" I queried again.

"Indeed, I did!" she said indignantly. "He came round and saw me and then he spoke to the youngsters. I saw him. And I saw the rude gesture that Matthew made in my direction, too, when Martin wasn't looking. In fact, I've called Martin several times but he tells me that he's never seen them do any of the things I've mentioned. It's true they've stopped playing pranks on me — but the more recent noises are worse! Oh dear!" Miss Basset put her head in her hands and sobbed.

"Can you describe these recent noises?" I asked when her shoulders stopped heaving.

She raised a tear-sodden face to me. I had seldom seen anyone look so overwrought.

"They're just terrible. Sometimes I think I'm going out of my mind. I thought it might be rats — but if it is they must have hobnailed boots on." She attempted a watery smile. "All I want to do is to watch my television in peace. Is that so much to ask?"

She looked as though she were going to cry again so I asked quickly: "Can you tell me where these noises are coming from?"

"As I said, the sounds seem to come from underneath the house. Footsteps cross the sitting room again and again. But there's no-one there. Nothing to see. I wonder if the house is haunted?" Miss Basset stopped speaking, and her knuckles whitened as she gripped her handbag even more tightly. "No, of course it can't be. The Reverend assured me there was nothing untoward in the house. I ask you! No wonder they call me names."

"Do you have a cellar?"

"No."

I frowned. "You're sure?"

"I've lived there twenty years. I'm sure there's no cellar."

"You live close to the church, don't you?" She nodded. "I've heard that the churchyard is riddled with old smugglers' tunnels. Do you know anything about that?"

Beatrice allowed the ghost of a smile to cross her face. "Yes, my mother used to tell me all about them."

"Do you know whether any of them ran close to your cottage?"

"All I know is that my mother remembered there being a passage that led into the cellars under our cottages when she was a little girl. She lived in Fleece Street then, and she and her friends used to play in the old passages and cellars. But she said they were all filled in after the War."

"And you've *checked* that there's no cellar under your cottage?" I pressed.

That strange smile again. "My mother and I hoped there might be. We used to make country wine and a cellar would have been the perfect place to store it. We looked everywhere but we never found an entrance."

"What about your neighbours? Do they have cellars?"

"One side does, I know. But not the other."

"Who lives in the one without a cellar?"

SOLICITING FROM HOME

"It's empty. So is the one next to it."

"Has it been empty for long?"

"No, only since James Watson died about three months ago."

"And there were no noises when he was alive?"

"Well … we could sometimes hear him coughing."

"Did you hear his footsteps?"

"No, I don't think so. Not like these anyway."

"What's the difference?"

"These are slow, lumbering and very heavy and … a sort of jangling." She shuddered. "You'll think I'm mad — but it sounds like chains. As if someone's feet are chained together. There! I've said it! It sounds like someone in shackles." She tried a tremulous smile but it was lost in the trembling of her whole body.

"Goodness me!" I exclaimed. "Are there any other sounds?"

She hesitated. "Yes. This will sound even more stupid, I know. I sometimes hear a scraping sound as if someone were dragging something heavy. Or perhaps rolling a barrel. But you must think …"

"I think someone is trying to scare you very badly," I said firmly. "The question is: *why?*"

I assured Miss Basset that I did not think for one moment that she was mad, informed her that I would do my best to find out who was trying to frighten her and why, and gave her a cup of hot sweet tea to drink.

The tea had an effect that was quicker and much stronger than all my promises. Beatrice's shaking stopped and her sweet smile peeped out.

"I can't thank you enough," she said after the first sip. "Not just for listening, but for wanting to help me."

"Don't mention it," I replied airily. "I'm sorry it would not be appropriate for you to apply for the injunction you wanted."

"Would it have been very expensive?"

"Yes," I told her. "And difficult to enforce. Anyway, it's not an option in the circumstances you have outlined to me. So let's put all that to one side and concentrate on the present problem. I'm beginning to think that Jimmy and Matthew aren't to blame for the latest noises. Perhaps there's a very different explanation."

"What explanation can there be?" She sounded more eager and animated than I had heard before. "Please tell me."

"I'd like to do a little research first, Miss Basset, if that's all right with you?"

"Yes, yes. Anything! I just want it to stop."

"And if it doesn't? What would you do?"

The smile slipped and she was instantly back to trembling and twitching from nose to fingertips like a frightened mouse.

"I don't know. I don't know. I've nowhere to go. No-one to stay with. I've no brothers or sisters — no relatives at all. All I own is the cottage which my mother left to me."

"You own the freehold, then, Miss Basset?"

"Yes, so the Council can't help."

"No, I understand that, but have you thought of selling?"

The tears returned, running unheeded down her cheeks. "The cottage is all I've got." I passed her a box of tissues. She

SOLICITING FROM HOME

took one, dried her cheeks and essayed a smile. "If I sold it, where would I go? It's not worth much, but it's mine!"

I put my hand over hers — the one that still held the soggy tissue. "I'm sorry if I've distressed you, but I needed to know."

"Oh, Mrs Russell," she breathed. Two spots of colour had appeared high on her cheeks and her breath came fast and shallowly. "Sometimes I think I'll die of this. My heart goes that fast and sounds that ragged, sometimes I think I'll have a heart attack. Doctor says they're palpitations and has given me some medicine. But nothing helps when I'm frightened."

I clasped both her cold hands in my warm ones. "Don't worry, Miss Basset, I'll find out what's going on, I promise. Would you like another cup of tea?"

She declined but the ordinariness of the question seemed to restore her spirits. When she took her leave, she was smiling.

Parts of our conversation came back to me throughout that day and into the night. Rather like learning my catechism, there were parts of it that were perfectly clear to me, but others that were hidden in mystery.

I knew that part of what troubled Beatrice could have been youngsters picking on her, but there seemed to be no real motive, other than that she was elderly and a little eccentric. I felt sure that a word from Martin would have been sufficient to put a stop to such behaviour. I was acquainted with the boys she had named and, while I knew they were high-spirited, I could not believe they would be so consistently unkind and annoying to someone so vulnerable. There had to be another explanation. That explanation had been in my mind while I was interviewing Beatrice, but I was loath to believe it.

In the end I decided to sleep on the problem. I did and woke with precisely the same explanation I'd thought of before I went to bed. All I had to do was prove that I was right — and that was the difficult part.

'Okay, first things first,' I told myself.

'Very well,' myself replied. 'But what *is* the first thing to do?'

'Seems to me that you need to go and inspect the property.'

'Why?'

'Stupid! That's where the noises are.'

'So?'

'Is she tormented anywhere else?'

'No.'

'Why not?'

'I don't know!'

'Think about it then. God! This is like drawing teeth.'

'Ah! I get it! It must be something to do with her home.'

'At last you're beginning to think like a rational person.'

'Meaning?'

'As you know, if one person picks on another their behaviour isn't usually limited to a single locality.'

'No, that's true. I get the point. What you're saying is that these youngsters would be mean to Beatrice whenever they see her. Not just when she's closed the curtains for the evening. Which is when most youngsters will be at home doing their homework or watching television or whatever else they do these days.'

'Now you're getting there.'

SOLICITING FROM HOME

'They wouldn't want to go out late just to play at ghosts to frighten Beatrice Basset.'

'Who said anything about ghosts?'

'Isn't that what you were implying?'

I sighed, fed up to the back teeth with myself and this frustrating internal dialogue. 'Go and check the place, Melanie. You might discover something. And if not, at least you'd know what other questions to ask!'

- 15 -

Beatrice's house was one of the terraced medieval cottages that ranged round two sides of the churchyard, which was roughly triangular in shape, the main road curving round the third side. I walked along the High Street towards the church and struck across the churchyard on the path that Beatrice had mentioned. At the far end, a group of youngsters were hanging around, some on bicycles, others sitting on a low wall, smoking.

They moved to let me pass, their eyes cast earthwards, except for one who smirked at me, his eyes narrowing.

"Hello," I greeted him. "Can you direct me to number 3 Lavender Cottages, please?"

The youngster was short and well-built, half sitting on a bicycle on which he was rocking to and fro in a manner that was somehow intimidating.

He jerked a thumb over his shoulder. "Third on the left."

"Thank you."

As I set off in the direction he had indicated, I heard a snort. I looked back and saw the little gang in a huddle around the boy. They were all facing me; there were some low-voiced comments I did not quite catch and a lot of sniggering. 'Just kids being objectionable kids,' I thought as I continued on my way, paying them no further attention.

"Hey! Mrs!"

The shout halted me in mid-step. I looked over my shoulder as the boy drew his bicycle into the kerb beside me.

SOLICITING FROM HOME

He thrust his face close to mine and the stench of cheap tobacco hit my nostrils. Instinctively I took a step back.

"If you're looking for Beatrice," he said, with what I took for a sneer. "She's not there."

"How do you know?" I asked without thinking.

"I just know," he said sullenly. "We keep a look-out for her. She's a bit soft in the head. Doesn't know which way is up. Tells us off all the time — says we do things just to frighten her."

"Really?" I asked, my nose climbing a little too high for politeness. "And is she right, by any chance?"

"We can't help winding her up, but she's okay really, is Beatrice."

I realised that what I had taken to be an unpleasant manner was, in fact, an adolescent combination of arrogance and diffidence.

"Why do you wind her up?" I asked, curious. To my surprise, he flushed and his eyes sought the road, but he kept pace with me. My suspicion from the night before grew stronger. "Were you paid to do it?"

He jerked to a stop and raised his eyes to mine. "Who told you?" he asked ingenuously.

"No-one," I admitted. "But I had my suspicions. And you're not the only one are you, Jimmy?"

He stopped in amazement. "You know my name!"

"Yes, and Matthew Denton's. You both come to the Youth Club, don't you?" He nodded shyly. "You do know that Miss Basset is really badly frightened? You should be ashamed of yourselves!"

I was half-expecting him to spit an invective my way

and shoot off on his bicycle, but he didn't. He had the grace to look shame-faced, his eyes dropping before mine.

"We don't do it no more. She thinks it's us, but it ain't. Not now."

"You said you keep a look-out for her. Why's that?" I asked, softening my tone as I walked on.

He kept pace with me, scooting along on his bicycle.

"She's still really scared by something."

"How do you know she's scared?"

"Policeman told us, asked us to look out for her."

"Oh, I see." Beatrice had said Martin had spoken to the youngsters. "And you say she's not at home now. Where is she, do you know?"

"Nope," he said. "Usually she would have been to the church by now. We ain't seen her at all."

"I'm Mrs Russell," I told him.

"Yes, I know."

"And you're Jimmy Gibbs, aren't you?" I asked.

"Yes, Mrs."

I turned to face him. "Tell me, Jimmy, who put you up to scaring Miss Basset in the first place?"

He turned sulky, thrusting out his lower lip and dropping his eyes again. "Some bloke we'd never seen before — nor since."

"Are you sure about that?" He refused to look at me, but nodded. "And you have no idea who he is?"

No answer. We had reached Beatrice's door. My escort turned the front wheel of his bike, about to turn back.

"Wait!" I demanded. "Shouldn't you be in school?"

SOLICITING FROM HOME

"Nope, Mrs Russell," he shouted over his shoulder as he pedalled away fast. "It's half term."

"Of course," I shouted back, knowing I had been rather ungracious. "Thank you for your help."

I was grateful for Jimmy's information, such as it was, but I knew Beatrice was expecting me and I didn't think she was the sort who would forget about our appointment. No doubt that was the reason she had not gone to the church.

Beatrice's cottage was the third in a line of three: so, technically, it was semi-detached. As she had said, the one at the far end was obviously empty and had a dilapidated air about it. The one next to hers was in better condition and looked as though it might still be occupied, judging by the flower-filled front garden and the half-open curtains at the windows.

Like its neighbours, Beatrice's front door was of thick oak, banded with brass. Its brass ring handle also served as a knocker. Beside the door hung a doorbell, an old-fashioned affair with a pull handle. I pulled hard and heard the bell jangling away inside but no-one came to the door. I tried again. Still no response. What next? Dare I peep in the window?

Putting one foot across the bed of lavender that ran under the bow window of the front living room, I peered in. Heavy lace curtains crossed inside but there was a tiny gap through which I caught a glimpse of a tidy, rather shabby parlour. It was empty.

There was nothing for it but to try the door again. Grabbing the round brass knocker, I struck it hard. To my surprise the door gave, swinging open to reveal a passage, the walls half-boarded and the floor covered in a rug that had seen better days.

"Hello!" I called. "Hello? Miss Basset? Beatrice? It's Melanie Russell. Are you there?"

I waited for what I thought was a minute before I called again. "Hello! Hello? Miss Basset?" My voice echoed slightly in the hall: Miss Basset did not seem to be in. Concerned, I peered into the front room and the one behind it but both were empty. As I was approaching a door at the end of the passage I heard the slam of what I presumed to be the back door. A flustered Beatrice Basset opened the door in front of me.

"I'm so sorry, Mrs Russell. I … I was visiting the privy."

She retraced her steps and I followed her into the kitchen where she proceeded to wash her hands thoroughly in the butler's sink by the back door. I presumed she used that sink for what my mother called 'dirty' jobs, because another shining enamel sink shone whitely in the sunshine streaming through the window. The whole house was comfortably shabby and seemed as clean as a whistle, tidy and well-organised.

"What would you like to see?" Miss Basset asked, drying her hands on the roller towel that hung on the back door.

I smiled. "I'd like to see the room where you notice the noises most."

"That would be in here." She led the way into the small living room at the front of the property. "In the parlour here and in the dining room behind."

"Do you hear anything upstairs?"

She shivered involuntarily. "Yes, in the small hours, when it's very quiet outside. The noises are louder then."

SOLICITING FROM HOME

She trembled and I noticed the pulse beating wildly in her neck at the recollection.

"Perhaps because they reverberate, do you think?" I suggested as she led the way up the winding stairway.

"I don't know. All I know is that, being all alone, I find it very fright ... fright ... frightening." Her brow glistened with sudden moisture and her hands clenched. I reached out towards her, but she turned before I touched her and led the way into the back bedroom which, I calculated, was above the dining room. "I sleep here. The front bedroom was my mother's. I can't bear to change it."

I let my hand drop. "How long do the noises continue?" I asked, looking round the small bare room that seemed devoid of personality, and noting that her narrow bed was set against the party wall that divided her cottage from the empty house next door.

Beatrice ran the tip of her tongue round her lips and her voice quavered: "It's odd. They go on for about twenty minutes, and then stop. Quite suddenly. Then there's silence. I feel my heart pumping in my ears. I lie awake and listen. I might even manage to go to sleep. And then it will happen again." Again I noted the involuntary clenching of her fists.

"Am I right in thinking there's no particular time when the noises happen?"

"Yes — and no. I mean, they seem to start when the sun goes down. Once or twice perhaps before I go to bed. I turn the telly up and try not to hear. Sometimes I even manage it if I'm watching something very interesting." A watery smile enlivened her features but faded quickly. "This is my mother's room."

It was a shrine. The neatly made bed endowed with a

thick satin eiderdown, the dressing table, with its mirror set at just the right angle, the pots and potions laid out, the silver-backed hairbrush and comb, the polished furniture, the vase of flowers on the chest of drawers, all spoke of devotion that now had no real purpose. My breath caught and tears pricked my eyes. I blinked them away hurriedly.

"What a beautiful room! I can see how much you loved your mother." This time I reached out and touched her upper arm and she didn't move away.

"Yes. I miss her greatly." The thought of her mother seemed to steady Beatrice. "*She* wouldn't have been scared. And I wouldn't be either, if she were still here." Beatrice let her hand touch the old woollen dressing gown that was carefully draped across the bed. Then she squared her shoulders, sniffed hard and walked back to the stairs.

I followed her into the parlour, where she turned and smiled. "And this is where the noises are loudest." Her smile crumbled and was gone. "Oh Mrs Russell, I'm at the end of my tether! What *can* be done?"

It was a cry from the heart. And although I wasn't sure if anything could be done, I was determined to find out exactly what it was that was causing Miss Basset such distress. As I stood there, uncertain what to say next, it dawned on me that we were standing close to the wall adjacent to the empty property next door.

"And this started after your next door neighbour died?"

I didn't expect the expression of horror that leapt into her eyes as her lips sketched an 'oh'. Realising that she'd jumped to the conclusion that I was suggesting the property was haunted by her erstwhile neighbour's ghost, I was quick to reassure her.

SOLICITING FROM HOME

"I am just wondering if someone is squatting there and trying to scare people from investigating." Far from calming her, this utterance had the opposite effect. She looked terrified.

"You think someone is living there illegally? Who? Some drug addict? Oh my!"

"I'm sorry, Miss Basset. I had no intention of worrying you. I was simply thinking aloud."

"But who could it be?"

"*If* it *is* anyone, I'll find out. Have no fear. But in the meantime I have a few more questions I'd like to ask."

"I'll do my best to answer."

"You said that the boys made faces at you through the window and left dog excrement everywhere. Is that still happening?"

"No, Martin made sure that stopped."

"So now it's the sound of heavy footsteps, jangling chains and something being moved?"

She inclined her head wordlessly, her cheeks suddenly as white as a summer cloud. I patted her arm reassuringly and as I did so I noticed that I was still holding a leaflet that I'd picked up from the front doormat on my way in. "I found this on the doormat," I said handing it to her.

Two round spots of red appeared on her full cheeks. "I wish they'd leave me alone. I receive one of these almost every day. I keep telling them I have no intention of moving but they keep on sending them."

"May I have a look?" The leaflet took the form of a large postcard advertising a firm of estate agents and asking whether the property was for sale. They assured the householder that they had a long list of prospective purchasers for her type of property.

"Do you know these agents?" I asked, frowning. I had noticed that they were not from Oldchurch. Everything seemed to be over-commercialised these days and estate agents had no compunction in leading the way.

"Not really — but they did come and put up a 'for sale' notice on my garden gate about a month ago. I told them I was not selling but it took a long time to get them to take it down. They said it was to advertise the property next door, but they didn't put it up *there* — and no-one's had the courtesy to tell me anything."

"Do you have the key to the next door property?"

"No, but the window's a little loose. I know because I saw my cat go through it."

"And is your cat here now?" I asked, looking round.

"No, he's usually sleeping in next door's garden." She shuddered.

"Shall we go and see if we can find him?" It seemed the perfect excuse to look more closely at the next-door cottage.

Miss Basset drew back. "Oh no, it's private property. I couldn't do that."

Her reluctance acted as a spur to my hot-headedness. "Perhaps you could make me a cup of tea? I'll go and take a look round the outside of the property next door."

I suited the action to the words and left the room. I felt her hesitate before she turned towards the kitchen.

- 16 -

Leaving Beatrice's front door ajar, I walked down the short front path to the pavement and stood for a moment surveying the cottages next door to Mavis' house. The small front was full of colour and the scent of flowers. Sweet Williams, sweet peas, Canterbury bells and hollyhocks made a wonderful cottage garden display, the latter casting shadows against the latticed window to the front room. I trailed my hands against the plants as I trod the three paces to the front door, banged a knocker very similar to Miss Basset's and waited. Although the place was bathed in bright sunshine, a sudden shiver ran up my back. Something made me turn round. Jimmy and a companion were staring at me from the road.

"There ain't anyone there, Mrs," said Jimmy.

"Are you sure?" I asked.

"Old man who lived there died a few months ago."

"Yes, Miss Basset told me."

A sudden scuffling noise behind me made me swing round. The door had opened, apparently by itself, because there was no-one to be seen. Hearing a snigger from the road, I swung round to find not two but three mischievous pairs of eyes looking at me.

"Okay," I said. "So which of you has been inside the house?"

"Us?" they asked in unison, eyes wide in mock-ingenuousness.

"Yes. I wasn't born yesterday. One of you was inside the

house just now and crept out while the others distracted me. Which of you was it?"

All three looked at each other and decided to brazen it out. "What's it to you anyway?" questioned Jimmy.

"It's all right," I said. "I won't tell on you, provided nothing's broken. What have you been doing in there?"

"Nothin'," came the sullen answer. "We ain't done nothin'."

"Why were you in there?"

Jimmy scuffed his foot against the pavement, looking down and away from me. The others mounted their bicycles and made for the corner of the churchyard at high speed.

"You can tell me, Jimmy. I promise you won't get into trouble."

"We saw a bloke go in there a while ago. We watched, but we didn't see him come out. We thought we'd find out what he was up to."

"I expect it was the estate agent."

"No, it were someone as we hasn't seen before. We know the agent. *Everyone* knows the *agent*." Scorn edged his voice.

I stood irresolutely on the doorstep. Should I go in with Jimmy watching my every move? Or should I retreat and have a look round the back of the property instead?

'Don't be a sissy!' I said to myself. 'You can't let a twelve year old boy decide your actions.'

I pushed the door wide into a hall that was the mirror image of Beatrice's.

"Is anyone there?" I asked loudly. Silence. Then a thump and a rustle disconcerted me. I stepped back just as a black and white cat scooted out of the door and along the path. Another thump. Curiosity got the better of me and I went in,

SOLICITING FROM HOME

calling "Hello? Hello? Is anyone there?"

Inside, the cottage was as cool and dark as it was hot and bright outside, its atmosphere damp and sinister. Goosebumps lifted along my arm. Crash! I jumped at the sound of something large crashing to the ground in one of the rooms above me.

My heart was still pumping when my ears caught an odd sound nearby. A cough. A rasping cough, cut short. A quick glance into the front room confirmed its emptiness, only the shadows of hollyhocks disturbed the sunlight that glittered on dust motes floating in the air. I moved on to the small back room which, empty and dark, reeked of damp.

The kitchen was similar in size to Miss Basset's, but there the comparison ended for every surface — floor, shelves, cupboards — was covered in piles of neatly-folded newspapers: in some places the piles reached from floor to ceiling. Strange. The newspapers must have been collected over a period of several years, but it was clear they had never even been opened. The meticulous stacks indicated a tidy, if weird, mind; there was a single path through them, leading to a small clear space where the cooker stood next to the sink. So Mr Watson had been able to cook and wash dishes but not to open his back door, for it was completely hidden behind a wall of newspapers.

I realised two things: it was as well that I had not tried to enter by the back door; and one of my pet theories — that someone had been entering that way to scare Miss Basset — had to be discarded.

I quickly shut the kitchen door and put a foot on the first stair. As I did so, a sense of dark despair descended towards me, filling me with apprehension, and so charged with emotion that it knocked me off balance physically. I stumbled. Recovering, I admonished myself.

'Be brave. There's nothing there. Everything has an explanation.'

I forced myself to climb the stairs although every nerve in my body was screaming at me to stop. The dark feeling became blacker, thickening until I found it hard to breathe. Holding my breath, I paced quickly from room to room. Each was empty, but the back bedroom was so thick with despair that it felt as though the walls would burst.

I rushed back down the stairs pursued by the uncanny feeling that I was being overtaken by evil, and was about to bolt out of the front door when I remembered the reason I had come in the first place.

My eyes rapidly scanned the hallway for a way into a cellar. I pulled open the door to the under-stair cupboard and sure enough, there was a trapdoor. But the feeling of impending doom had thickened so much that I could not bear to stay a moment longer or to investigate further.

I flew towards the front door. Realising as I reached it that I might have an audience, I stopped suddenly. I took a quick breath to collect myself before I stepped over the doorstep and pulled the door closed behind me.

Sure enough, Jimmy was waiting for me. I smiled at him and he frowned.

"You all right, Mrs Russell?"

"Yes, I'm fine," I lied.

"Didn't you feel it?" he asked in puzzlement.

"Feel what?"

"*Death*," he said. "We reckon that's what it is. *Death*."

"Reckon what is?"

SOLICITING FROM HOME

"Did you *really* not feel it?" Not wanting to admit that I had, I simply looked at him questioningly. "It feels really dark and spooky in there. That's why we dare each other to go in."

I smiled. "So it was a dare? Nothing more?"

He looked at me suspiciously. "What do you mean?"

"There was no man, was there? It was simply a dare."

"No, no," he protested. "There was a man and we didn't see him come out."

"So it was a double dare?"

He frowned. "Yes. But Johnny says there was no-one there, anyway. No-one but the ghost that is!"

"Ghost?"

"He said he heard a thump and didn't wait to hear no more. But he was sure the place was empty. So what happened to that man?"

"He must have come out when you weren't looking," I suggested. "I'm sure there's no-one there. I looked in all the rooms."

"It's a puzzle," he said frowning. "I'm sure he ain't come out. There's no way he could've got out the back door. Not with all those papers stacked there."

This utterance convinced me that he had been inside the cottage himself— perhaps it was worth asking another question.

"I didn't go down in the cellar. Have you been down there?"

"No fear. It's bad enough upstairs! None of us have been able to stay in the place more than a few minutes. Though I was in there the longest," he bragged. "Three and a half minutes. Even Johnny could only manage two minutes fifty

201

seconds." He paused, considering me with what could have been approval. "Even *you* were in there less than five minutes. Four minutes five seconds — I timed you." He indicated the stop-watch on his wrist. "Whatever you say, I reckon you felt it."

I smiled deprecatingly and walked towards him. "What should I have felt?"

"It's spooky in there. Old Mr Watson hanged himself, you know. In the back bedroom. It's dark and haunted." He lowered his voice to a whisper and continued: "You can hear the crash as the chair falls over and the last gasp he ever made."

"Nonsense," I said crisply as I walked back into Miss Basset's lavender scented garden. "And by the way, Miss Basset *is* at home."

I knocked gently on Beatrice's door so as not to startle her. "It's only me, Miss Basset," I called, opening it to find her standing in the hall with a beautifully laid tea-tray in her hands.

"Let's go into the parlour." She nodded towards the door into the front room and followed me in, setting the tray on a small table by an old scuffed-but-comfortable-looking leather armchair that faced the window.

"Do sit down," she said, indicating what could only be the visitor's chair — a beautiful armchair covered in flowery chintz with a snowy antimacassar pinned in place on its back.

"It's Earl Grey," she said. "Do you prefer milk or lemon?"

"Neither, thank you."

"Ah, my mother always said that was the right way to

SOLICITING FROM HOME

drink it." She passed me a blue and white bone china cup and saucer, both rimmed with gold, that I recognised as Spode. I noticed a small chip on the teapot's spout as a drop of tea landed on the snowy white tray cloth. Beatrice hurriedly moved the bowl of sugar cubes to hide it.

"Did you find anything next door?" she asked passing me a matching plate of biscuits and an embroidered napkin.

"Thank you." Placing my teacup down on a side table to allow the tea to cool, I selected a custard cream biscuit from the plate. "I'm afraid not. Jimmy thought that a man had gone into the place and it's true the door was ajar. I called and went in. But I didn't see anyone."

"You went inside? Oh! You shouldn't. There's something peculiar about that place. The last two people who lived there committed suicide. I'm not a nosy neighbour but I do like to be friends and I've never been invited in. I wouldn't go in there now if you paid me! Why did you?"

Luckily I was given time to answer this query by the simple fact that I was munching my custard cream. I weighed up in my mind whether I should tell her of my suspicions, wondering if my thoughts would only make her unduly nervous. I opted for the truth.

"I have a feeling that someone is trying to frighten you into selling your cottage. I hoped I'd find some evidence."

"They were hoarders you know, Mr and Mrs Watson senior *and* Mr Watson Junior. It was full of stuff. You wouldn't believe what I've seen come out of there since he died."

Remembering the piled newspapers, I could believe it, but said nothing. I took a sip of my tea to give me time to think. I knew that I wasn't prepared to investigate further on my own. It was time to tell Beatrice's tale to the local policeman and ask him to search the property.

"It certainly has an unpleasant atmosphere," I remarked.

"Unpleasant atmosphere?" Miss Basset chattered on. "So it isn't just me being silly? You felt it too. I was always saying to mother that we should ask the Reverend to visit and bless the place, but she always said we couldn't do anything. It was up to the Watsons — but now they're all dead. Do you think I should ask him?"

"I think that would be a very good idea. It might help to put your mind at rest."

"Oh I'm so glad you said that. I shall speak to the Reverend this very afternoon."

"I wonder if it would be all right with you if I asked Martin to have a look round as well?"

"Would you? I'd be so grateful. I don't want him thinking that I'm completely off my rocker but if *you* were to ask him …"

"In that case, I will." I finished my tea, stood up and passed the empty cup and saucer back to her. "In fact, I'll do it now."

Having said my goodbyes, I made my way straight to the police station where I was lucky enough to find Martin on duty, scratching his head over paperwork. I explained the situation and confided my fears to him.

"I'm afraid it's not a police matter, Mrs Russell. It's a civil matter, not a criminal one."

"But, surely, if she's being threatened…?"

"Is she being threatened, Mrs Russell? Is anyone threatening to beat her up, rob or murder her? The short answer is 'no'. From what you tell me, she is imagining noises. I'm not surprised because I know she's highly strung. But I've already done all I can."

"I know you asked the youngsters to keep an eye out for her. And it seems they do. But surely she shouldn't be pressured into selling her house?"

"As I understand it, a firm of estate agents have asked whether she wants to sell her property. That's a perfectly legitimate question."

"Yes, but…"

"Look, Mrs Russell, I have a lot to get on with." He sighed and waved a hand at his overladen desk. "Look at this lot! Much as I'd like to help, it's not a police matter."

I left him and made my way home, vowing to myself that I would not let the matter rest and annoyed that so far I had discovered nothing and that Martin had refused his help. Poppadum was delighted to see me and, in our usual fashion of greeting, I scooped her over on her back and tickled her tummy. When she'd had enough I grabbed her collar, attached her lead and we walked back along the High Street to collect Sarah-Jane from Olive, who'd been looking after her for me. I determined to ask Olive, who was always a mine of local knowledge, whether she knew anything about the dead Mr Watson and his house.

And, sure enough, she did.

"Funny family, that," she said. "A family of depressives with all sorts of other problems. They were hoarders, kept *everything* in case it would come in useful. I suppose you would call it an obsession. In the end Social Services came along and insisted that they clear the house because it was becoming a health hazard. Neighbours were complaining of rats. And the Watsons were becoming very whiffy because they had things stored in the bath — you know, that sort of thing."

"I do indeed! I've had to clear all sorts of properties when the owner has died."

"Oh, I didn't realise you did that sort of thing."

"Not often, but sometimes there's no-one else — and if you're the junior assistant solicitor, it often becomes your duty."

Marigold gave me an odd look as if she only half believed me, and went on with her story.

"As I was saying …. Old Mrs Watson fought Social Services tooth and nail but it was no good, everything was removed from the sitting room, apart from the furniture. And when that was found to be rat-infested and full of woodworm, Social Services cleared that away too. The next thing we knew, Mrs Watson was gabbling like a madwoman. So back came Social Services. They carted her away to an old folks home or something. She never came back."

"I suppose the sudden change turned her mind?"

Olive shrugged. "Probably. Or maybe she was already over the edge when they took action. Next thing we heard, she'd slit her wrists and died. There was hell to pay, as you can imagine."

"Oh dear. What happened to her husband?"

"He was the next casualty. You see it was old Mrs Watson that kept the family going and he couldn't bear it when she left. Didn't know what to do. The place was filthy and full of stuff again in no-time. Social Services apparently despaired, kept calling round, organising clearance and generally interfering. Old Mr Watson couldn't take it. Eventually he saw them off with an old shotgun. Lord

SOLICITING FROM HOME

knows where he found it — probably under a pile of rubbish."

"That must have put the wind up them!"

She looked at me soberly. "Yes, but Social Services came back, of course — and this time they had a Court order for him to be detained in a mental institution, so they brought the police with them. Old Mr Watson danced about in front of them with his shotgun, threatening to shoot. The police didn't think the gun was loaded but, when they tried to take the gun from him, all of a sudden he stopped yelling at them, put the barrel in his mouth and pulled the trigger. They knew it had been loaded *then*, by gum! Blew his brains out."

"Oh my word! How terrible!"

"The shock had a lasting effect on their son, Peter, who was near fifty years of age. He never spoke again. He closed himself up in that house and seldom came out — except to go for long, long walks and tend the garden, which was always his pride and joy. The garden and his dog, Bonzo — a small funny-looking mongrel — were his only pleasures. In the summer he would walk for miles with Bonzo but he never spoke to anyone and often forgot to eat. His neighbours looked out for him, especially old Mrs Basset. She would leave food for him on his porch. He was never quite right in the head, but harmless."

"I'm not surprised. What horrible ways to lose his parents."

"Yes, but he was never quite right in the head even before they died. It was always the three of them. They were never apart until they took his mother away."

"What a sad story."

"And it gets worse. Bonzo was run over by a car — some say on purpose — but we'll never know because the driver didn't stop. Peter saw it happen, picked the dog up and carried him into the garden, cradling him in his arms, stroking and caressing him and whispering to him. The story goes that the dog licked Peter's hand — and died. A neighbour called the vet, but Bonzo was already dead when the vet arrived."

"Oh no! This is getting even worse."

"Peter seemed to deal with the dog's death calmly enough. People said he didn't shed a single tear. He buried Bonzo in the garden. After that Peter wasn't seen for weeks. In the end, Miss Basset called the police who found him hanging from the hook holding the light fitting in the back bedroom. The Coroner's verdict was suicide. The sad thing is — the front door was unlocked. Anyone could have found him, but they'd learned to leave him alone, so no-one tried."

"That's not a sad story, it's a tragedy," I commented.

Although the sun was still shining with its summer brilliance, the light seemed to have dimmed. No wonder 2 Lavender Cottages felt so full of hopeless desperation.

Sarah-Jane whimpered in my arms and I realised I'd unconsciously tightened my hold on her. I looked down into her little face, usually so rosy and smiling, but now puckered into a frown, and thought again how blessed I was. She mouthed at my bosom.

"She's hungry," said Olive. "You arrived just as I was about to give her a bottle. Would you like to feed her here?"

"Yes, thanks," I said and settled down to nurse my baby. Olive sat down on the settee opposite, smiling at us in contemplative fashion. After a short while of peaceful

SOLICITING FROM HOME

absorption in our respective thoughts, she said: "Odd that you should mention the Watsons. I've been hearing rumours that the place is haunted. Never heard that before."

I pricked up my ears. "Haunted?"

"Yes, apparently haunted by something dreadful — probably from old smugglers times. Groans and cries and the sound of barrels rolling and chains jangling. Mind you, that was what Jimmy Gibbs told my Andy, so it's probably just boys' bravado."

"How did Jimmy come to hear of it?"

"You know how silly boys can be? Well, there's a few of them that like to frighten each other with silly ideas — my Andy's one of the gang — and one of them dared Jimmy to stay overnight in the Watsons' place. Apparently he couldn't resist the dare, so that evening at home, he went to bed early at about eight o'clock saying he didn't feel well, then slipped out of the window and was away."

I grinned. "I can just imagine that!"

She smiled and sighed. "As I said: boys!"

"Do go on."

"Apparently, Jimmy made a camp in the front room of Number 2 and settled down with a comic and a torch. It was just getting dark when he heard the noises, apparently coming from somewhere below him. I don't think it was long before he scarpered!"

"Really? He *really* heard noises?"

"He must have done. His mother said that he rushed straight into their front room, as white as a sheet, with chattering teeth. Looked round wildly. Then dashed upstairs. When his mother went up she found him cowering under his bed clothes! Not that I'm supposed to know, of

course."
 "Interesting," I said, and left it at that.

- 17 -

I was pushing the pram home along the High Street pavement when I stopped in my tracks and turned back the way I had come. Poppadum looked up at me as if to say: 'make up your mind, won't you?'

I patted her head and said conversationally: "Sorry old girl, I've changed my mind. I've decided there's no time like the present and if Martin won't take a look at the property, I'll just have to go on my own."

Within five minutes we were outside 2 Lavender Cottages again. Of Jimmy and his friends there was no sign and I breathed a sigh of relief. I wanted to do this as quickly as possible, preferably without an audience. I felt my heart quicken in anticipation as I wheeled the pram up the short path and parked it beside the front door.

"Stay here, Pops," I commanded. "On guard!"

The dog heaved a great sigh and laid down by the pram. I knew I could trust her to take care of Sarah-Jane who was happily fast asleep. "I'll be as quick as I can, I promise."

I cast my eyes along the road to check that there was no-one around. Two rows of cottages were dreaming in the sunshine, their front doors firmly shut and their windows obscured by lace curtains. I watched to see whether any of those curtains twitched but they all hung still and limp. Glancing at Miss Basset's property I saw that its door was closed. For a split second I wondered whether I should let her know what I was about to do, but instantly decided against it. What would be the point? I had worried her enough for one day. And, anyway, I needed to do this quickly or not at all.

'Stop dithering, Melanie!' I said to myself — and with that thought I twisted the iron handle. To my relief the door opened smoothly and quietly. How fortuitous! Leaving the door open to give me some light, I ran into the hall, opened the cupboard under the stairs and stopped dead. I was certain that I'd seen a trap door in the floor on my last fleeting visit, but it seemed to have disappeared. The remembered atmosphere of dark despair surrounded me, absorbing the light from the doorway, making my pulse race and my breath shorten. I registered all this while my eyes raked the floor. Not floorboards, like the hall. No, this floor was covered in something. Lino? Yes, linoleum. My fingers traced the edge, found a worn place, curled under and pulled. Up came the linoleum, and there underneath was the trap door. Frowning, I realised that someone had been in the property after I'd left. Of course! The man whom Jimmy and his friends had seen entering the property. They'd said they hadn't seen him leave. Perhaps he'd been down in the cellar. Please God, he had gone now. I had no idea how I would explain my presence if he suddenly appeared and challenged me.

All these thoughts raced through my mind as I raised the trapdoor, leaned it back against the wall and felt around for a light switch. I was beginning to think there was no electric light fitted in the cellar, and was wondering whether it would be sensible to leave and come back some other time — remembering to bring a torch with me next time — when my searching fingers came across the switch they were seeking and flicked it on. A dim light bulb illuminated the

SOLICITING FROM HOME

space below and a wooden ladder that stood against the wall below the trap. Grabbing it, I descended fast and my skirt caught on something — a nail perhaps; I heard it tear but paid no attention, being fully occupied with my somewhat precipitous descent. On reaching the floor, I stood still, allowing my eyes to adjust to the dim light. Two things were clear — it was a sizeable cellar, stretching away to both sides of the trap, and for that reason it stretched under the party wall that divided this cottage from Miss Basset's. So there *was* a cellar under her property even though she had no access to it. That meant that the noises which so disturbed her might well emanate from this dungeon.

Reason insisted there must be a rational explanation for the noises, and I could think of only one. Someone wanted to frighten Miss Basset, probably into selling her property for a song, and was prepared to use foul means to achieve this end. The 'foul means' was most likely a tape recording machine — and that was probably something to do with the man whom Jimmy had seen.

Swiftly checking along the walls for a power point, I came across the tape recorder I was searching for. A brief glance informed me that it was attached to a time switch. All was now clear: I had guessed correctly.

A dog barked. I recognised the note of warning. Poppadum! I lost no time in retracing my steps, replacing the trapdoor and the piece of linoleum, closing the door to the cupboard and running back down the passage to the front door. There I stopped abruptly.

Poppadum was barking fiercely and Sarah-Jane was screaming. Over the pram, just out of Poppadum's reach, bent a figure. Beyond, a few people had gathered near the gate and I noticed a good deal of curtain-twitching across the road.

My heart in my mouth, "Miss Basset!" I said loudly as I closed the door behind me. The figure started and turned towards me with a look that combined surprise with relief.

"Oh, is it your baby, Mrs Russell?"

I managed a smile. "Yes." I picked up the yelling bundle and held her to me. Her sobs subsided into a hiccough and calm was restored. The few people round the gate began to disperse amidst mumbles and smiles, until only one person was left — a short dark man of portly build, dressed in a brown suit, white shirt, beige tie and shining tan shoes. He stood motionless at the gate, his bottom lip thrust out and a deep frown on his face, looking the picture of annoyance.

Suddenly, he stepped forward and confronted me, thrusting his face so close to mine that I involuntarily drew back.

"And what have you been doing, young woman? You know you're trespassing? This is private property, I'd have you know." His breath was foul with cigarette smoke. I drew back, finding myself speechless even though I had rehearsed an excuse for my actions.

"This is my solicitor, Mrs Russell," came a wavering voice that became firmer as it went on. A transformation came over my nervous client: she drew herself up to her full height, a good four inches smaller than my five feet eight, acquiring a certain stateliness in the process. "I am Miss Basset and I live next door at 3 Lavender Cottages. Mrs Russell is acting on my instructions. Who, may I ask, are *you*?" She looked down her nose at the man, whose demeanour changed considerably: he became all oily amiability.

"Harry Prendergast. Call me Harry," he introduced himself, thrusting out a hand to my champion. "I own this property — and the one next door. I've been wanting to meet you, Miss Basset. How do you do?"

"How do you do?" she replied automatically, as manners required, and from courtesy her fingertips touched his, but dropped away hastily.

"I won't beat about the bush. I want to buy your cottage."

"As I have already told your agents, I have no intention of selling."

Oily Man's face changed into a supercilious smirk. "Really? We'll see about that!" he muttered.

"And I certainly would not sell it to you. I do not think much of the way you treat a lady. I have no wish to speak to you further. If you have anything you wish to convey to me, kindly instruct your solicitor to contact Mrs Russell."

She turned and walked back towards her front door, leaving the oily man trying to school his scowling features into blankness. "Come, Mrs Russell," she ordered, glancing at me over her shoulder. "We have matters to discuss."

Amazed at my client's sudden self confidence and still unusually tongue-tied, I followed her, still holding Sarah-Jane and pushing the pram — and thus Poppadum — with my free hand. I glanced at Mr Prendergast as I passed him, but his eyes were fixed on Poppadum who snarled nastily in his direction. As she came abreast of him, he took a hurried step back and shot me a look. I saw that I had made an enemy.

Far from upsetting me, I felt the steel return to my

backbone and with the full intention of adding insult to injury, I smiled at him triumphantly as I entered Miss Basset's domain — although I also left Poppadum outside guarding the pram. It was just as well that I'd regained my aplomb because I found Miss Basset again prey to her nervous nature, sitting in the front room trembling from her clasped hands to her crossed ankles.

After I'd thanked her for her timely appearance and intervention on my behalf, I lost no time in telling her what I had discovered. Astonishment turned quickly to bewilderment, from there to annoyance and thence to dismay. I watched the changing emotions cross her face and felt obliged to say:

"Please don't worry, Beatrice. I spoke to Martin and he told me that this was a civil matter and not a criminal one. He said there was nothing he could do — which is why I decided to do my own snooping. Martin is right — this is a civil matter and I know just what to do."

"You are sure that those noises are only recordings?"

"I'm certain. I'm glad we've found that out, but I am very cross that anyone should try to scare you like that."

"The worst thing is — they succeeded. Oh, I feel so foolish!"

"It's easy to say that when you know what the situation is. It's quite a different matter when you're alone and grieving and someone intentionally tries to scare you in the middle of the night. You have been very brave. And very sensible to take legal advice."

"Why do you think someone would want to scare me?"

"Unless I'm very much mistaken, I believe that they were going to try and drive you out of the house so they

SOLICITING FROM HOME

could acquire it at a price which is less than its value. If Mr Prendergast already owns the other two cottages in this row, as he says he does, then I'm certain he has his eye on this one too. The whole row would make a wonderful single house, or could be redeveloped. Either way, someone would stand to make a large profit."

"But who? You don't think it was that man outside, do you?"

"From my viewpoint Mr Prendergast seems to be the most likely candidate — but only if he can acquire your cottage for a knock-down price."

"The bully! Is there anything you can do about it?"

"Indeed there is. And I shall! But only if you are happy with that, of course."

"Please tell me."

"The legal term is 'the tort of private nuisance'. I intend to have strong words with Mr Prendergast's agents. And with his his solicitors. I shall ask for an injunction to prevent them doing anything which may cause a nuisance to you...."

She looked relieved. "Thank you. Yes, please go ahead."

I smiled I hadn't quite finished. "And I will ask for compensation ... in fact, punitive exemplary damages ... for the anxiety and fear you have endured."

And that is exactly what I did.

Although it took some months before I was able to reach a satisfactory settlement with Mr Prendergast's solicitor, I did obtain a temporary injunction within two days. The injunction expired within a fortnight, but it had done what had been intended. No further attempts were made to unnerve Miss Basset.

To my surprise, it turned out that Mr Prendergast had been entirely unaware that someone had been trying to frighten Miss Basset into selling her cottage. I believed him because, after his initial anger had settled, he went out of his way to soothe Miss Bassett's fears.

I was still convinced that someone had been trying to obtain Miss Basset's cottage at an undervalue. I determined to get to the bottom of the affair. I began by making discreet enquiries.

I learned from Jimmy that he and Matthew had been paid the huge sum of five pounds by a young man to 'play jokes' on the nervous woman. When Martin, the policeman, had taken them to task, they had stopped their tricks immediately, but had had insufficient courage to own up. Instead they had kept an informal watch.

As Jimmy had told me, they'd seen the stranger enter the next-door cottage. Jimmy gave a detailed description of the fellow, swearing he was different from the young man who had bribed him and Matthew.

The estate agents in charge of the sale, Messrs Byitt & Seed, angrily denied knowledge of any such person. So did Mr Prendergast and his solicitors. They all denounced such behaviour, insisting that if someone had acted so despicably it was without their knowledge, and certainly without their consent, tacit or otherwise.

All my later enquiries were unproductive until, eventually, Messrs Byitt and Seed admitted that a key to the front door of 2 Lavender Cottages was missing from its keyring. When I asked they had no idea when it had gone or who had taken it. Privately, I wondered whether this lapse

SOLICITING FROM HOME

in memory had been caused by the fact that Mr Prendergast had given strict instructions that anyone viewing the property should be accompanied by one of the Agents' staff.

In vain did I write stiff letters demanding reparation, followed by softer ones demanding an explanation. For two weeks there was none to be had. Then one of the negotiators remembered that his sister had covered holiday leave for the receptionist.

I asked for her name and address and soon discovered what had happened.

"I was on my own in the office," she said. "I couldn't leave."

"You're not in trouble, I promise," I reassured her. "I'd just like to know what happened."

"This man came in. He was in a hurry, he said. He was looking for a holiday home to purchase, and 2 Lavender Cottages looked perfect. I tried to phone Mr Byitt, but he had left the office. I tried. I really did!"

"I'm sure you did. So what happened next?"

"He was really pushy. I took the keys down and looked at the label. I told him he had to be accompanied if he wanted to view the property." She looked stricken.

"But, of course, you couldn't leave the office."

She looked relieved that I understood. "I suggested he came back later. But next minute he just grabbed the keys out of my hand and was gone."

"Poor you! I bet you were hoping he'd bring them back quickly."

She nodded. "Luckily for me, he did. Popped them back on my desk while I was doing some photocopying."

"How much later was that?"

"Couldn't have been more than half an hour."

"I don't expect you had time to take his name and address?"

"No." She hung her head. "I know I should have done, but he brought the keys back. I was so relieved, I just hung them back in the cupboard. I knew the property was empty. He couldn't have stolen anything."

"Quite."

I thanked her and left. Another dead end. What a pity. I comforted myself with the thought that at least Miss Basset had discovered a rational explanation for the noises she'd heard.

I thought that would be the last I heard of the intruder, but Fate was still playing with me. Enter Mr Green.

Mr Green instructed a firm of estate agents to make an extremely low offer for Miss Basset's property. At the same time, Mr Green made Mr Prendergast a very low offer for both the other cottages. Both offers were rejected out-of-hand. Miss Basset had no intention of selling her property, and Mr Prendergast considered the price offered far too low to warrant serious consideration.

Two days after Beatrice refused the offer, a middle-aged man with a loud suit and a scornful expression knocked on her door. Barely had she opened it, than he wedged his foot over the threshold.

"Why did you refuse my offer, you silly woman? You'll never get another half as good."

Beatrice blinked, but stood her ground.

"I presume you're Mr Green?"

He ignored her question, and leaned forward with a

SOLICITING FROM HOME

grimace that was as menacing as his words.

"Have you looked at your cottage recently? The roof's rotten. There's rising damp here under the windows. And no doubt there's deathwatch beetle in all the beams."

"I presume you're Mr Green?"

"What if I am? It won't make any difference to this hovel you call a home! Look at this! Like I said. Rotten with damp."

With the words he pulled hard at the doorframe. When it didn't budge, he took out his car keys and scored a line down the paint.

"There!" he said, "See that?"

Beatrice peered in the direction he was pointing. "You've marked the paintwork."

"It's rotten, see?" He dug his fingers in and this time a piece of the frame came away.

"Oh!"

Mr Green ignored her. He dropped the piece of wood, stepping back and sucking air through his teeth as he gazed upwards at the roof. "Yeah! Definitely deathwatch. Never get rid of it. Eats right through the beams. Roof'll fall in any minute." He stepped back a bit further. "Chimney's leaning, too."

The teeth-sucking became noisier. "That'll cost you. Over a thousand pounds I reckon. You'd be an idiot not to take my offer."

Beatrice, feeling intimidated, said: "What offer?"

"Two thousand pounds. I suggest you take it, or else ..."

Anger was overcoming Beatrice's fear. She stood still, feeling it build, saying nothing.

"Well? I'm waiting for an answer!"

"I have no intention of replying to someone so uncivil."

"Uncivil?" he'd sneered. "I'll give you uncivil!"

He raised his fist, threateningly. As Beatrice closed the door his knuckles slammed into it.

At this, Jimmy, who, as usual, had been keeping an eye out for Miss Basset mounted his bicycle and rode fast to the police house. When he returned with Martin, Mr Green was beating on Miss Bassett's front window. Martin hauled Mr Green off to the police station, where Jimmy swiftly identified him as the man whom he had seen going in and coming out of 2 Lavender Cottages on the morning I found the tape recorder. In the end, Mr Green admitted his guilt, confirming he'd intended to frighten Miss Basset into selling her property to him.

Miss Bassett was generous in victory, refusing to press charges. Mr Green was soon released from custody and, fortunately for him, he was never again seen in Oldchurch.

Not long afterwards, Mr Prendergast instructed his solicitors to write to me, extending an 'ex gratia' payment to Miss Basset. Of course, the payment was made solely as evidence of his good faith and without any admission of liability. But it was a kind gesture, and one that relieved Beatrice of her immediate financial worries. Mr Pendergast went up in my estimation, as well as in hers.

Although the noises had stopped, Beatrice was still aware of the feeling of hopeless black dejection that pervaded the next-door cottage. Worse, she believed the bleak depression was leaking into her own home. So she was delighted when, some weeks after my correspondence with his solicitors had elicited the ex gratia payment, Mr

SOLICITING FROM HOME

Prendergast contacted the Rector and asked him to perform an exorcism at 2 Lavender Cottages. His reason, he said, was that all prospective occupiers, whether potential purchasers or possible tenants, had been repelled by the cottage's chillingly dark atmosphere. The Rector was pleased to oblige and, at Miss Basset's request, I attended the ceremony.

Soon afterwards Beatrice Basset made peace with Mr Prendergast, the latter now a much-chastened individual. Within days he arranged for the painting of the exterior of the two cottages he owned, magnanimously paying for the exterior of Miss Basset's property to be repaired and decorated at the same time.

About a year later, I received in the post a silver envelope addressed to Mr and Mrs Russell. When I opened it I was astonished to find an invitation to the marriage of Miss Beatrice Basset to Mr Henry Prendergast. I had heard rumours of romance blossoming between the unlikely couple, but had smiled wryly, thinking I knew better.

While I was wondering whether the invitation was mere courtesy or whether they both really wanted me at their nuptials, the telephone rang.

"Please come," Beatrice said. "Harry and I think of you as our personal cupid. Just think — without you we would never have met. And I would never have found my back bone!"

The wedding took place in Beatrice's beloved church which was filled to overflowing with flowers, music and well-wishers. My lingering doubts were soon dispelled by the happiness that shone from the bride's face and the gentle, considerate expression on the groom's.

Beatrice's smile lit up her face as she welcomed her guests to a lavish reception spread out in the large dining room of the single house (now known as Prendergast Place) that Harry had converted from the three Lavender Cottages.

The atmosphere of Prendergast Place was so warm and comfortable that I found it difficult to remember the feeling of dark despair that had so affected me in the Watson's cottage, nor the grief that had surrounded Beatrice in the home she had shared with her mother.

I found myself smiling for days after the ceremony. But alas! I have to admit that Harry and Beatrice's wedding was the first and last time in my long legal career that a dispute between neighbours was so happily resolved.

- 18 -

By eight o'clock in the morning the sun was shining from a misty azure sky: by nine-thirty the sun was hot and the sky a clear summer blue, without a cloud in sight.

I heard the Quarter Boys of Rye church clock strike the three-quarter hour as I climbed the steep cobbled street, unsteady in my platform-soled shoes. I was garbed in a conventional black suit and white blouse so at least I looked like an advocate even though I didn't feel like one. I seldom appeared in court because I usually dealt only with non-contentious matters. Feeling nervous and sticky, I turned the corner into Market Street, and almost collided with old Mr Turner, the very senior partner of a Solicitors' firm in Rye.

"Good Morning, Mrs Russell. What a pleasure to see you here! I thought you'd deserted the law in favour of motherhood?"

"How could I desert the law?" I smiled in response. "You're right, of course. I did take time off to have a baby, but I seem to have started my own practice already."

"Congratulations, my dear. Is it a girl or a boy? And where is he or she?"

"A daughter, Sarah-Jane. I've left her with my long-suffering mother, although I do have a baby-minder. I didn't think Mr Dart would approve of me bringing a baby into the courtroom."

Mr Dart was the Clerk to the Justices, a dour man who

oozed self importance. As the Justices' Clerk, he administered the Court and explained the law and legal procedures to the Bench. The Bench was usually made up of three magistrates, or justices as they were also known. Not being lawyers, they relied heavily on Mr Dart for advice: a fact of which he was only too aware.

Mr Turner's lips curved in a smile which lighted up his lined countenance. "What are you here for, my dear?" he enquired.

"I'm representing a client who's making a licensing application."

"Liquor licence, I presume?"

"Precisely."

"Wouldn't be for 'The Monk's Abode' by any chance?"

"Funnily enough, yes."

By this time we had crossed the road and were about to enter the Town Hall, the whole first floor of which comprised an ancient courtroom. Mr Turner caught my arm.

"A word to the wise, my dear. Since it's a restaurant, no objection to your application can be sustained provided that alcoholic beverages are sold with food."

"Yes, I…"

His long-suffering look silenced me. "But we have an old lady who comes to every licensing application to object on temperance and religious grounds. She does her best to put a spanner in the works, which is a great nuisance. But she speaks from a place of conviction and the Magistrates have no course open to them other than to hear her."

"But…"

"Simply allow her to make her objections. The Magistrates will grant your order afterwards, but it will save

SOLICITING FROM HOME

you losing face by trying to shut her up."

"I see. Thank you for the advice."

He held the door open for me as I entered the ancient Town Hall. My client, Mr Palmer, was waiting for me. A tall, slim, dark-haired man, he was attired as though he was still in the Edwardian age, in a dark suit with a waistcoat and fob watch. I was already feeling the heat after the effort of walking up the hill, and looking at him in his buttoned-up suit made me feel even hotter. He came towards me with both hands extended. His demeanour was coolly polite and his face expressionless as he bade me good morning in a deep voice bowing over my extended hand with 'olde worlde' courtesy.

I explained the procedure for his application to the Court, to which he responded with a sardonic smile. He still looked cool. I moved away to check the Court list and found that Mr Palmer's case was listed close to the bottom of the Licensing Applications. I warned him that he might have to wait a while, shook his hand, and walked into the courtroom.

I seldom represented a client in Court so my appearance there was noticed by the other advocates, all of whom were men. As they made space for me on the advocates' table, I was aware of a buzz of whispers along the line. Heads turned. I took my place feeling discomforted although I did my best not to show it.

Ahead of me, on their raised bench, sat the Magistrates. I felt the Chairman's eyes boring into me. I turned my head slightly and saw him looking directly at me, eyes narrowed and mouth pulled into a straight line. He turned to his neighbour, and to my relief I saw that he was smiling. He motioned to Mr Dart and muttered something to him. Much to my surprise, the next moment my hearing was called.

I took a deep breath and stood up. I introduced my application to the Court, relieved that my voice sounded firm and low despite my performance anxiety. After outlining my application, I called my client to give evidence. The Court Usher echoed my words.

Mr Paul Palmer strolled to the witness stand and took the oath in a cool and detached voice.

"Please give your full name and address," I said.

He complied.

I had hardly completed leading him through his evidence — in which he had confirmed that all necessary notices had been served and that no objections had been received — when a diminutive woman of indeterminate age jumped up from a chair at the side of the Court and demanded to put some questions to him. A collective sigh of anticipation hushed along the row of solicitor advocates. The solicitor next to me grinned sardonically. I jumped when the Chairman addressed me.

"Have you completed your questioning, Mrs Russell?"

"Yes, Sir."

"Then you may proceed, Miss Ferguson."

The Magistrate smiled in a long-suffering manner, waved the small woman to a place before him and sat back in a pose of resignation. Miss Ferguson, appearing to be completely at ease, gave her full name as Miss Violet Eileen Ferguson and her address.

"I object to this application in the strongest terms," she announced.

SOLICITING FROM HOME

Light hair, neither blonde nor grey, straggled from a bun at the nape of a neck that was a little too long for her body, so that her head jerked forward like a moorhen's when she moved. She was clad in a shapeless green two piece suit and a pair of sensible but scuffed brogues. A pair of handsome grey eyes glanced round the Courtroom and came to rest on mine. She frowned slightly before turning to Mr Palmer, who was now lounging languidly against the edge of the witness box.

"Do you believe in God, sir?" she asked.

Mr Palmer raised his eyebrows at me. I looked down.

"Do I have to answer that?" he asked the Magistrate.

"It would be helpful. If you'd be so kind."

Mr Palmer shrugged laconically. "Not particularly," he said, directing this utterance towards Miss Ferguson.

"But you just swore on the Bible!" The little woman's head bobbed accusingly.

"Yes."

"But you don't believe in God!"

"I did not say that. My words were *'not particularly'*."

There was a ripple of interest along the advocates' bench. I thought I detected a gleam of amusement in the Chairman's eye.

"That indicates that you are not a believer."

"You should draw no such conclusion."

"What conclusion should I draw?"

"I have absolutely no interest in your drawing any conclusion at all from my words."

"How can one *'not particularly'* believe in God?" she asked caustically. "One either believes or one does not believe. I believe you do not believe."

"That is *your* belief. It is not mine. In fact, *I* do not particularly believe *your* belief."

All around me, I detected restrained amusement at this unexpected war of words. Should I intervene, I wondered? Instantly realising that any effort of mine would be clumsy compared to Mr Palmer's skilful handling of his adversary, I relaxed, deciding to enjoy the verbal sparring.

Miss Ferguson resorted to drama.

"You are foresworn! You swore on the Bible by Almighty God," she declared, pointing an accusatory finger that trembled alarmingly in unison with the agitated jerking of her head.

Mr Palmer raised his eyebrows once more, sighed and responded. "I swore the oath required of me."

"But if you do not believe in God, then your oath has no value."

My client looked from her to me and back again. He shrugged again, and sighed dramatically. A long deep sigh.

"So you agree that your oath has no value?" The little woman was like a terrier snarling over a bone.

"Don't be ridiculous, my good woman. Of course my oath has value. I am a gentleman."

"That has nothing to do with my question."

"I agree. A gentleman always agrees with a lady when possible. What *was* your question?"

"I asked if you believed in God. I asked if you agreed that your oath has no value." The terrier had been replaced by a cat, playing with a mouse ... but this mouse was about to get away.

"I replied that I do not particularly believe in a particular God. I said I did not agree that my oath was invalid. I do not necessarily believe that every word in the Bible is true, but I believe that it contains truths."

"That is splitting hairs."

"Not at all. I have my own beliefs — and one of them is that *you* have no right to question me on those beliefs."

I thought it was time I intervened. I stood up. The Chairman waved me back into my seat before I could open my mouth.

"Sit down, Mrs Russell. Your client has no need of you."

Miss Ferguson was determined. She tried again.

"Do you believe in God? That's a simple question. Yes or No?"

"My dear woman, I am here to make an application for a liquor licence for my restaurant, not to be examined on my catechism."

To say that this was like a red rag to a bull would be an understatement. Miss Ferguson paled, then reddened and paled again. She pulled her shoulders back and drew herself up to her full height — of about five feet, I guessed — struggled to control her facial expression and eventually said coldly: "Please read this."

She handed Mr Palmer a piece of foolscap paper, closely typed.

"Do I have to?" My client asked the Magistrate plaintively.

"If you would."

The tall man applied himself to the task with ostentatious assiduousness. A minute later he looked up, and silently passed the paper back to Miss Ferguson.

"There. I've read it."

"Do you ...?" she began.

"I've read it, as you asked."

"It says there that ..."

"Yes, I've read it."

"As it says there ..."

"Yes, I know. I've read it." He looked beseechingly at the Bench. "Do I have to answer questions on it, your Worship?"

"No, you don't." The Magistrate was struggling not to smile. "Do you have any other points to put, Miss Ferguson?"

"Yes. That leaflet shows ...." Miss Ferguson launched into a long harangue about the evils of liquor.

My neighbour leaned over and whispered. "Aren't you going to shut her up?"

I debated with myself whether I should try. The solicitor on the other side of me gently prodded me with his elbow, rolled his eyes and motioned me to get up.

The objector was just getting into her stride. According to her, the demon drink was the sole cause of crime, not to mention all sorts of other noxious, offensive and infectious behaviour.

I rose, thinking that I should demonstrate some support for my client. No-one appeared to take the slightest notice of me. I cleared my throat.

Miss Ferguson was in full flow now. Apparently the granting of a liquor licence was against the tenor of the Ten Commandments.

I cleared my throat again, more loudly.

Miss Ferguson stopped speaking long enough to swallow.

"May it please you, Sir ..." I started.

The Chairman shook his head, his hand indicating that I

SOLICITING FROM HOME

should sit down. I caught Mr Turner's eye. He winked at me.

I sat. Mr Palmer looked at me, shrugged and looked down, unable to hide an ironical smile.

The objector licked her lips. She raised her voice to assert that the grant of a liquor licence was against the tenets of the Methodist Church, the church of which she was a member and which was situated adjacent to 'The Monk's Abode'.

Her address to the Court ran on in similar vein for another few minutes, during which time I swear she took not a single breath. When she finally ran out of words, the Chairman inclined his head to her.

"Thank you, Miss Ferguson. We have listened to your objections."

He looked along the Bench. His fellow magistrates were nodding dutifully.

"I hope you agree that you have been heard?" He did not give her time to answer before continuing. "As you know, we have listened to your objections several times in the past, on similar occasions, in similar cases when you have objected on similar grounds. No doubt, you are therefore already aware that the Bench has no alternative but to grant the licence that is the subject of this application. The proper notices have been served and the Police and Fire Brigade have raised no objections to the grant of the licence. You may be comforted by the fact that the licence will permit alcohol to be served *only* as an adjunct to food."

His eyes gleamed again as he added: "I sincerely hope that this will prevent any undue drunkenness or any of the extreme behaviour which you so much fear."

Miss Ferguson raised her eyes heavenwards, but did not

say anything more, much to my relief.

Turning to Mr Palmer with a genuine smile, he continued. "Your Application is granted, Mr Palmer. And may I commend you on your eloquence? If you were to turn your hand from the restaurant trade to that of advocate, I have no doubt but that you would have great success. You may leave the stand now."

I smiled my thanks to Mr Turner as, with great relief, I gathered up my papers, pushed my way between the other advocates and escaped into the foyer. Mr Palmer was waiting for me.

"I'm glad you warned me, Mrs Russell," he said. "That was the last sort of questioning I was expecting this morning."

"I'm sorry I couldn't prevent it," I apologised. "But at least you have your licence."

"Yes." His straight face broke into a smile at last. "And a good story to go with it."

He shook my outstretched hand, inclined his head to me and left the building.

- 19 -

And so the long hot summer continued, seemingly without end. The passing of each day was marked by some small change in my baby: she learned to suck her thumb, to smile, to laugh, to shake her fists, to kick her legs, to push herself up. Her back strengthened and soon she was sitting up by herself. She put on weight and grew prodigiously. Before long she knew to smile at her father and say 'dad… dad…dada' when he came in from work. She learned, too, that I would give her anything if she remembered to mumble 'mum…mum…mum'.

Although she was the light of my life and I loved her to distraction, I loved being my own boss, too. I found my work absorbing and interesting and I enjoyed keeping my brain and my body active, and feeling useful to others as well as to my family. I also relished the opportunity to be of service to my community.

So, as day followed day, I grew in experience. I met many people and learned many things. I made plans for my practice and gradually they came into being, not without certain struggles and setbacks, but through them I learned the way of the world and lost the rose-coloured lenses to my spectacles. I learned to look beneath the surface and to realise that all was not as it might seem. Beneath the smooth surface of the millpond of normality, strong cold currents of opportunism or criminality often ran deep. In short, I matured professionally and, I believe, became a respected member of the legal profession.

Melanie Russell

Sometimes, I was weighed down with the responsibility of acting for others, but in times of stress or when the whole world seemed destined to be against me, I would take refuge in a beautiful memory:

I awoke in the middle of the night feeling warm and contented, infused with gratitude for all that my life held. Moonlight flooded the room and a gentle breeze stirred the curtains: I crept to the casement and looked out into the garden. Truly it was a night made for dreaming contemplation – a white night, full of the moon and the magic of the moon. Her silent luminous light shone down on me through the whispering new leaves of the willow and apple trees, chequering the shadows with silver and turning the stream at the bottom of the garden to a path of pewter made for the feet of fairies. As I stood staring at the moon's pale loveliness, there was borne to my nostrils the scent of flowers, herbs and the dewy earth; while from the mystery of the little wood beyond the brook stole the soft, sweet song of a nightingale.

Acknowledgements

First I would like to acknowledge my debt to my parents, Betty and Harold Chapman, now long dead, who brought me up to love and honour my fellow man and woman, to acknowledge the beauty of the natural world of which we are all part, and to treat all around me with fairness and kindness. It was they who instilled in me a love of honour, ethics and professionalism.

I acknowledge the debt owed by the public to my profession in its continual struggle to uphold the Rule of Law — even in the oldest democracy in the world.

The beauty of Romney Marsh is held in the heart long after a person leaves its vicinity. The spell cast by its wide open skies and broad flat land lingers in the mind, providing an inner space where one can breathe freely, emotions are calmed and creative endeavour stimulated.

I am grateful beyond measure to those, many of whom have now passed away, who helped me to set up in practice on my own account at a time when a young lawyer who was also a woman, a wife and a mother, was a rarity.

I thank my clients, too numerous to mention individually, who were prepared to take a chance by instructing a young female lawyer and who taught me much about the ways of the world.

Every young mother needs a dog, and dear Poppadum was there to teach me how to bring up babies by providing a perfect example of intuitive motherhood when she gave birth to ten puppies not long after my first daughter was born.

Special thanks go to those dear people who have been my helpmeets in the production of this book, my beta readers, my editors, above all my friends: Christine Warrington, Vivien Ford, Richard Eaton and Tricia Oakland, all of whom read the manuscript more than once and made suggestions that have enriched my prose. With sincere thanks, I salute you.

I am grateful to David Hobbs for the wonderful illustration for the cover which so well evokes the special magic of Romney Marsh, and to Matt Maguire of Candescent Press for the cover design and formatting of the e-book version of 'Soliciting from Home'. Their respective web-sites are: www.davidhobbsillustration.com and www.candescentpress.co.uk.

But most of all, thank you, my readers, for lending your eyes and ears to my story. I do hope you enjoyed reading it.

About the Author

Melanie Russell has wanted to write a memoir about her first days in practice on her own account for many, many years. Several attempts ended up in the waste paper basket: others were kept for inspiration. Forty years later, when the practice of the law has changed vastly, Melanie is delighted that she has finally managed to achieve this small goal.

She lives in the Sussex countryside with a very understanding husband, a very spoiled dog and a large rambling garden, all of which she manages to keep in some semblance of order.

A note from the Author

Thank you very much for reading my memoir. I do hope you enjoyed living and working on Romney Marsh with me. You may not know that honest reviews are of immense value to an author so if you would leave one at amazon.co.uk and amazon.com it would be of enormous help. It would also be greatly appreciated. Thank you.

Other Books Published by Touchworks Ltd.

Print & e-books available from amazon.co.uk & amazon.com

Getting Ready to START A BUSINESS
by Richard Eaton

REVIEWS

"The most relevant business start-up book I have seen. In a few pages it reminds the reader of essential points and provides links to best practice. An excellent work. One to read before you start and to keep on the shelf for future reference."
    CLIVE MARSH, Author
    Financial Management for Non-Financial Managers
    Business and Financial Models: Kogan Page

"A pocket-sized guide for aspiring entrepreneurs that links to valuable and reliable online information: a real help for those at the start of the business planning process."
    IAN SMALLWOOD, Head of Business Services,
    Let's Do Business Group

"Succinct points and clear advice in a neat package. If you are setting up your business this book tells you clearly the issues you face and how to start dealing with them. ... Great advice succinctly put, this guide sets out a clear framework, checklist and where to go next. It is useful for setting up any kind of business."
    CATH TAJIMA-POWELL, Arts & Heritage Project Manager

"Essential reading for anyone who wants to start their own business."
    CHARLOTTE ELFDAHL, Founder of Rockville Lampshades
    Winner of 'Tomorrow's Business Builders Award 2013'

"A handy guide providing good background information to help you with taking the first steps in researching your business and writing your business plan"
    KAYE CRITTELL of Let's Do Business Group

"A handy reference to guide you as you write your Business Plan and prepare to start up in business."
    KEIR DELLAR, Head of Projects,
    Let's Do Business Group

When the Clocks Stopped
by M.L. Eaton

No 1 in the Mysterious Marsh Series

The long hot summer of 1976. The mysterious Romney Marsh in the South of England. Hazel Dawkins, a feisty young lawyer, takes maternity leave anticipating a period of tranquillity. Instead, the dreams begin. In them she encounters Annie, a passionate young woman whose romantic and tempestuous life was adventurously lived, more than two centuries previously, in the cottage that Hazel now occupies.

As their destinies entwine, Hazel not only confronts a terrifying challenge which parallels history, she finds herself desperately fighting for survival in a cruel and unforgiving age. Even more disturbing is the realisation that her battle will affect the future for those in the past whose fate is, as yet, unwritten.

Her only ally is Annie. Together they face events that echo through the centuries, events that are as violent and compelling as they are unexpected.

And, as the past collides with the present, the time for the birth of Hazel's child draws ever nearer.

When the Tide Turned
by M.L. Eaton

No 2 in the Mysterious Marsh Series

It is August 1976 and an oppressive heat hangs over Romney Marsh in the South East corner of England.

Soon after the birth of her daughter, Hazel Dawkins, a young lawyer, is unexpectedly asked to return to work. No sooner has she agreed than she discovers that a dark force threatens both her family and her country; and before long, the past and present intertwine in a rising tide of horrifying events.

Haunted by terrifying images, she knows that she must uncover secrets from the past if she is to avert a catastrophe that will destroy all that she holds dear.

What draws her to the painting depicting a sudden storm at sea on a night in 1803 as Napoleon prepares to invade England?

What is the secret of the man pegged down to die on the incoming tide?

As Hazel seeks the answers to these questions, she faces evil and intrigue, her life and that of her baby daughter, threatened at every turn.

A Taste of

When the Clocks Stopped

Prologue

The silver light of a gibbous moon shimmers on the new green leaves of the ash tree. The horse stamps and jerks his head, jangling the bridle. I sway with the movement, soothing him instinctively. The sweetish smell of horse is thick about me as I wait at the crossroads. Stiff as I am in every joint and sinew, my body screams for me to dismount and stretch my legs, but I cannot. Some intuition, some sense of impending destiny, holds me motionless. I am aware it will not be long.

I flinch as the expectant hush is broken by the screech of an owl, eerie in the stillness that binds me to the saddle. She circles silently above me, seeking her prey. I watch until she glides away into the blackest shadows, where the sacred ash grove huddles beneath the escarpment.

My eyes seek the hallowed place where the Earth Mother is still honoured by man and maid on the sacred feast of Beltane; the ash grove to which they come at dawn, clad in white, and garlanded in green. May blossoms wreathe their brows as they stand side by side under a living canopy for their hand-clasping, their ceremony of rejoicing in union, the celebration of life itself in dance and song. This is the seven-treed sacred grove to which my beloved and I came not long ago; there we swore an oath to honour our love and there later, alone beneath the moon-silvered leaves we became one in the flesh.

It grows cold now, and I shiver. The horse pricks up his ears, listening intently. A small sound trembles towards me; perhaps no more than a fluctuation in the air current. Then the nightingale's exquisite song fills the air with beauty. It is the signal: Jack's signal.

I fire my weapon into the sky and wheel about, pulling

sharply on the reins. We race off into the night. Lying close to the horse's back, my head beside his ear, I ride hard. For a moment or two, as we gather speed, I choose those places where the low light gleams through the covering of cloud. I catch the sound of hooves in swift pursuit and know I have been seen. Now I guide my good companion into the gloom of the darkest shadows, allowing him to choose his own footing on the causeway. He gallops on.

I risk a backward glimpse. Shapes pursue us; legless in the mist rising from the Marsh, centaurs ride hard in a bow-shaped line. The triumph and excitement of the men who chase me is almost palpable. How long were they lingering near the crossroads where I myself had waited?

I let the gelding have his head because he knows these levels well. His hooves drum into the earth and I crouch low in the saddle, horse sweat hot-smelling in my nostrils. As I cling to his mane, I chance another glance but see nothing. I am sure we are gaining on our pursuers, but have they ridden yet into the trap where the Marsh is quicksand and will swallow horse and rider whole?

The moon is hidden now and I have no bearings. All I hear is a thrumming, thrumming, thrumming — and I know not whether it is my heart beating in my ears or the sound of pursuit. All I can do is ride.

Made in the USA
Charleston, SC
04 June 2016